In Praise of One-night Stand

AN OLD PHILOSOPHER'S SEXUAL MEMOIR

K. T. FANN

In Praise of One-night Stand
An Old Philosopher's Sexual Memoir

Copyright © 2022 by K. T. Fann.

Paperback ISBN: 978-1-63812-218-0
Ebook ISBN: 978-1-63812-219-7

All rights reserved. No part in this book may be produced and transmitted in any form or by any means, electronic, or mechanical, including photocopying, recording, or by any information storage and retrieval system, without permission in writing from the copyright owner.

The views expressed in this work are solely those of the author and do not necessarily reflect the views of the publisher hereby disclaims any responsibility for them.

Published by Pen Culture Solutions   03/17/2022

Pen Culture Solutions
1-888-727-7204 (USA)
1-800-950-458 (Australia)
support@penculturesolutions.com

It Takes Just One

I
Some big and some small
Some short and some tall
Some young and some old
Some hot and some cold
That's all just fine
For it takes just one
To turn the whole world upside down

II
Some weak and some strong
Some right and some wrong
Some good and some bad
Some happy and some sad
That's all just fine
For it takes all kinds
To make the world go round and round

III
Some day and some night
Some play and some fight
Some forward and some shy
Some ask how some ask why
That's all just fine
For it takes just one
To turn the whole world upside down

IV

Some wheel and some deal
Some cheat and some steal
Some bitter and some sweet
Some at home, some on street
That's all just fine
For it takes all kinds
To make the world go round and round

V

Some heavy and some light
Some loose and some tight
Some shallow and some deep
Some for now, some for keep
That's all just fine
For it takes just one
To turn the whole world upside down

VI

Some down and some up
Some go and some stop
Some push and some pull
Some wise and some fool
That's all just fine
For it takes all kinds
To make the world go round and round

VII

Some fast and some slow
Some suck and some blow
Some dry and some wet
Some cool and some sweat
That's all just fine
For it takes just one
To turn the whole world upside down

VIII

Some soft and some tough
Some cry and some laugh
Some quiet and some shout
Some believe and some doubt
That's all just fine
For it takes all kinds
To make the world go round and round

IX

Some buy and some sell
Some silent and some tell
Some use and some abuse
Some accept and some refuse
That's all just fine
For it takes just one
To turn the whole world upside down

X

Some give and some take
Some real and some fake
Some come and some don't
Some stay and some won't
That's all just fine
For it takes all kinds
To make the world go round and round

XI

Some love and some hate
Some luck and some fate
Some lose and some gain
Some once and some again
That's all just fine
For it takes just one
To turn the whole world upside down

XII

Some sow and some reap
some awake, some asleep
Some grateful, some regret
Some remember, some forget
That's all just fine
For it takes all kinds
To make the world go round and round

Foreword

I am an eighty-four-year-old retired philosopher. Twenty-five years ago I decided to follow my favorite philosopher Laozi's footsteps by retiring to my ancestral village in Taiwan and turning a one-hectare abandoned farm into my ideal retirement paradise. I planted some century-old trees and more than a hundred kinds of fruit trees. I have innumerable chickens, ducks, geese, peacocks, parrots, rabbits, and horses running free on my property. It's like a semitropical rainforest and I was as happy as a lark. Unfortunately, I was struck down by a stroke two years ago, which paralyzed my right arm and leg. My idyllic old farmer's life came to a screeching halt. Luckily my memory and other vital functions of the brain seem to be unaffected. I have no choice but to return to my previous scholarly life of writing books. I first spent about six months finishing my life-long unfinished project on Laozi, and then spent a lot of time turning my early philosophical books on Wittgenstein into e-books. Since then I have mastered the art of publishing e-books on Amazon's Kindle Direct Publishing and have published six short books on different topics ranging from "Food and Sex Are Hunan Nature" to "The Miracle of Vibration Therapy".

One book that's been lurking in the back of my mind for a long time is a book about sex. You see, abort forty years ago while I was going through a painful divorce, I decided to teach a course called "Philosophy of Sex" at my university. My other favorite philosopher Wittgenstein once said to his student: "What is the use of studying philosophy if all that does for you is to enable you to talk with some plausibility about some abstruse questions of logic, etc., and if it does not improve your thinking about the important questions of everyday life?" Other than the food, is there anything more important to everyday life than sex? Yet philosophers rarely discuss sex as a philosophical topic. I tried to apply my philosophical skills to help myself think clearly about the male-female relationships while living them. Over the years I have formed my own philosophy of sex and seriously contemplated writing a philosophical book, following my course outline with the title, "Thinking About Sex".

But such a book would be too didactic and boring. My recent writings convinced me that I write best when I let my thoughts range freely, and do not try to organize them into a set form. So there won't be a table of contents or chapter divisions in this book.

What follows are my sexual reminiscences interjected with my philosophizing about them. The events described are real and the persons involved are real, but with names changed. Some parts of it may sound to some people like pornography, but it is actually a philosophy book. A great contemporary philosopher Noam Chomsky said, "The job of a philosopher is to tell the truth and to expose lies." That's what I am trying to do. Another great philosopher Karl Marx said, "Philosophers hitherto have only interpreted the world in various ways, the point, however is to change it." I am also trying to do that. This is not just a memoir but I meant it to be a subversive track. I wish to subvert the status quo of our sexual mores. In fact, I meant this to be a Manifesto of Sexual Liberation!

Old People's sex

Before my stroke, I still had regular sexual needs. First, let me set the record straight about the sexual needs of the elderly. Like ordinary people, some people have strong sexual needs and some don't. I regard myself as someone with normal sexual needs, I assumed everyone else is the same. I was surprised, based on my classroom survey, to find out that about 5% of young men and women said they didn't feel the need at all. So, people have different sexual needs including the elderly. Most people assume elder folks have no sexual needs. That may be true of the majority, most likely because of the lack of opportunity and not ability. One of my neighbors told me this story about his father who lived to be 103. Once he took his 100-year-old father to the hospital to get a physical exam and afterward the nurse laughingly told him," Your father had an erection when I touched him!" He was overjoyed and arranged to take his father to a brothel. Most prostitutes were afraid to take him on, but finally, a foreigner took him on, and afterward reported that he could still ejaculate!

My two good friends were sex maniacs according to normal reckoning. The elder one who died at age 91 told me three months before he died that he felt his sexual prowess was declining for the first time. He felt his erection was not as hard as before and he had a hard time ejaculating.

At that time he had two girlfriends, sisters in their 30's, and they were playing three p's! The other friend was a real sex maniac also. I haven't met or heard of anyone else with such a strong libido. He had two lovers, one in her 70's the other in her 30's, living in different towns. I know as a fact that he visited each of them at least once a week, even a few months before he died of lung cancer at 84. What amazed me was, that wasn't enough for him. He told me he had to resort to masturbation sometimes, and that he still ejaculated as much semen as he did in his youth. That's incredible, as I noticed a definite decline in my libido since my mid-seventies.

After my stroke, my sexual desire vanished completely. Not only because it is physically impossible to do, but mainly because the fire within is totally extinguished, probably due to the many drugs I am taking to avert another stroke. Now that I am totally sexless, I can think about sex objectively and clearly!

Since my body is quite useless now, I cannot do the many things I used to enjoy doing. I am left with only my brain functioning. In fact, it seems to be functioning better than before, since I noticed a tremendous improvement in my memory. I remember things I couldn't remember before. I am a regular person with a regular long life which had its regular ups and downs. But as I reminisce about my past, I notice the most memorable events are the few one-night stands I had the privilege to have. Why? I started thinking and philosophizing. And here is my answer.

Human Nature

Humans are a kind of animal. As an animal, we are endowed with the two most basic functions: to live and to reproduce. These are programmed into our very constitution, our body. That's nature's way, that's Dao, that's God's command. Our bodies are designed for those purposes, and nature makes sure you do them by a simple pain-pleasure principle. When you are hungry you feel pain and when you eat you feel pleasure. When the time comes for you to reproduce, if you don't do it you feel terrible discomfort, and if you do it you feel pleasure.

Pleasure is nature's lure for individuals to engage in reproductive activity. And sexual desire is set by nature at a certain season for the best survival of the offspring, such as spring or rainy season. All highly evolved animals have sexual desire only during the mating season while they are of reproductive age. Reproduction is so tied up with sex we tend to think of it as the only purpose nature set for life. In fact many animals die soon after they perform their reproductive duty, especially insects.

Humans are a unique species, we have sexual needs all year round and all your lives, way past your reproductive ability. In humans sex is de-coupled from reproduction! Think about this! In Chinese there is a common saying, "Food and sex are human nature". Meaning: the need tor food and sex is the part of our nature we share with animals, but we are better, we have civilization, morality, religion, etc, that make us no longer animals. The denigration of our sexuality and elevation of our spirituality coincided with the rise of civilization and culminated in religion. All religions (with the sole exception of Daoism) regard sex as the biggest stumbling block on our way to spirituality, and consequently as something to be suppressed. There is a long and complicated story to be told here, but I only wish to register my dissenting voice here.

My view is that the most unique feature of human beings as a species is that sex is divorced from reproduction. It has become an independent realm of life activity for its own sake. It should be enjoyed as a uniquely human activity, and regarded as a basic natural human right. If you cannot enjoy sex for its own sake, you are not fully human! Unfortunately, for thousands of years under the so-called civilization, religion, morality, and social taboos have conspired to prevent humanity from satisfying this basic human need. From childhood, we are brainwashed to regard sex as bad, dirty, and immoral, and only becomes allowable in the most restrictive setup called marriage. I consider this whole process a crime against humanity and it's high time people rebel against it. Fortunately, even with this pervasive indoctrination, some people, sometimes, manage to breakthrough. And that's what *a one-night stand* is all about. For about ten years after my divorce, I was relatively free sexually and was lucky to have experienced a few one-night stands. Most people tend to think of it as immoral at worst or as something meaningless at best. But if I went to a convention,

I saw a beautiful woman, was terribly attracted to her and she was attracted to me also, we knew we would never see each other again, and decided to get together that night for sex. What's wrong with that?

Julia

That's exactly what happened one night in the 1980s when I went to Varna, Bulgaria to attend the World Congress of Philosophy. I stopped by Budapest to see my philosopher friend Agnes Heller who along with his teacher Lukas were been persecuted by the Communist government then. The next day I got on the plane going to Varna and sat next to a beautiful woman. I asked her where was she from and was she going to the philosophical congress also? She said yes and she was a philosophy student from the University of Budapest. I asked her, did you know Agnes Heller? She immediately burst into laughter. I asked why are you laughing? She said just yesterday her school authority called the philosophy students attending the congress together and told them specifically not to talk to anyone about Heller, and the first question the first person she met asked was about Heller!

So we both laughed and the only topic of our conversation on our short flight was Agnes Heller! Before we disembarked in Varna she asked, will I see you again? I said come to my session where I will be presenting a paper. I gave her my calling card and she gave me her name, Julia with the last name ending with "s". I learned then in Hungarian a name like the famous philosopher Lukas, you pronounce "Lukash" with the emphasis on "sh".

The next day she did come to my session and sat right in the front row. That was quite distracting as she was full-bodied with her bosom prominently displayed in front of me. I find myself particularly attracted to women's breasts. Why? I ask myself? Actually, it's quite simple. We are incomplete beings, we are born male or female. We each have missing parts only others have. We are naturally attracted to what you are missing. In addition, we all remember consciously or unconsciously the comfort and pleasure of suckling from your mother. Also when a woman is in the part of the monthly cycle when she can conceive, the breast swells and becomes larger.

Evolution has recognized this and exploits this by having men particularly attracted to a woman when the breast is large.

Julia was wearing a grass green chiffon dress and I swear I could see her nipples jiggering when she moved her bottom to adjust her seat. Oh my God, it took all my will power to bring my attention back to my paper. I could hardly wait until the session was over to take her to the reception dance party organized by the president of Bulgaria. After a glass of champagne, we got to the dance floor when waltz music was playing. I am not a good dancer, I barely know the traditional waltz. But I think it is the sexiest dance, for two of you are holding each other close, chest to breasts. That's really too much and should be banned! That night she did not wear anything under her thin chiffon dress, no bra, no underwear!

And that should be banned also! The bubbly had an aphrodisiac effect on me especially as it worked its way down my belly. I was going out of my mind! She must be feeling the same way, as she was holding me closer and tighter and I could feel her burning bosom.

So I asked her, "Where are you staying tonight?" She said, "With friends in the student's dorm". I said, "Why don't you accompany me tonight? I have a large nice room." She said OK and I said let's go! So we left the party to go to my room, and let her shower first. While she was showering, I asked if I could join her. She said sure. So I went to join her. My God what a sight to behold. She was like the painting of Venus coming out of her bath, except more alive and beautiful. I couldn't wait to run up and hold her in my arms and try to put my penis into her vagina. As I have not done this before, i.e. having sex while showering, I didn't realize there was a problem.

Vaginal Discharge

Let me digress here a little to tell you a fact about vaginal discharge or pussy juice in colloquial terms. We all know that when a man is sexually attracted to a woman a sure sign is an erection. But we, including women, don't know what's the physical sign of a woman being attracted to a man if any.

Well, I can tell you there is a sure sign—the woman will start flowing pussy juice. The reason is simple and natural. You see, when a woman is sexually attracted to a man, her body naturally prepares itself to receive his penis by lubricating itself first, otherwise, there is no way the penis can get in. From this fact, we can draw important conclusions about the male-female relationship. When a man wants to know whether a woman really wants to have sex with you, all you need to do is touch her vagina to see if it is wet and your penis can easily slide in. I notice in the drug stores there are a lot of vaginal lubricants for sale. That only means that there are a lot of dry vaginas in the world, a sure sign of a big social problem. If you are a woman and want to know whether you are really sexually attracted to a man, you only need to check your body to see if it is ready to welcome him when you are with him. The body has a life of its own, it doesn't obey your orders. You should learn to listen to it.

Getting back to my Julia, I could not get into her, not because her body refused me or the standing position was odd, but because her juice was washed away by water. In later tries with other women in a similar situation, I manage to get in by putting my saliva on my penis first.

The saliva is very similar to women's juice and a good emergency lubricant for intercourse.

So we both finished our showering, dried ourselves and she got in bed. Lying there she looked like the sculpture of an Indian goddess with especially prominent full round breasts. I hopped on the bed, started sucking her breast, and immediately popped my throbbing penis into her wet vagina. I was home! I felt like I was in the bosom of Mother Earth suckling. I was one with Nature. Look at the Chinese Yin-Yang sign. It consists of the female and the male embracing each other to form a full circle.

You are complete when you are embracing your other half!

I pity people who must take LSD, opium or who must meditate for hours to get a mystical experience. Here it is, easy and free, you just have to meet your other half Mother Nature has made for you. In theory that should be as easy as finding food when you are hungry, and that must be the case in our original state before the onslaught of civilization. But unfortunately, we invested so much extracurricular considerations into sex that it becomes the hardest thing to get. Julia and I were hundreds of miles away from home in a strange country, we were not encumbered by many unnecessary considerations. We were on our natural self, answering Mother Nature's call, enjoying our natural rights. You may ask, what about love in all this? This reminds me of a classic conversation in one of Woody Allen's movies. His girlfriend Diane Keaton says," Sex without love is really an empty experience." Woody Allen replied." You are right, but as far as empty experiences go, it's one of the best!" Life is full of empty experiences, but sex, especially a one-night stand, is one of the best. That's why forty years later it's still as fresh as yesterday in my mind!

Flora

Julia wasn't my first one-night stand. I was taking a pottery class in a community center. Here let me tell you something about these hobby courses such as pottery, dance, yoga etc. Most students were women. Those classes are the best place for men to meet women. There was this gorgeous black woman occupying the potter's wheel next to me. She had a profile like queen Nefertiti and sensual lips like Zain Asher at CNN and she was as black as ebony. She was always smiling and had the most hearty laughs. It was a joy just to look at her. One day she said, "Kuni, can you come over to show me how to throw a bowl? I am Flora." So I said, "OK Flora," and went over in front of her wheel to demonstrate to her. She said, "No, no, I can't learn that way. You should come behind me and show my hands how to do it." So I did as she said. While holding her hands from behind her I felt this special warmth and softness of her flesh. Let me tell you this secret when a woman feels sexy her body turns extra warm and soft. The feeling is unmistakable. As I was about to withdraw my hands she took hold of them and whisper, "You really turn me on!" I quickly returned to my seat.

The bell had just rung for the end of class. As I was preparing to leave, she came over and said," I am going to take the driving test tomorrow for my driver's license. Won't you take me to a parking lot to get some practice?" Of course, I said yes and took her to a large parking lot overlooking the lake. The view was breathtaking. I drove around the parking lot once slowly and explained what I thought were the key points she should know. Then I let her take the wheel. As it turned out she could drive perfectly well, the request for me to teach her was just an excuse, and after driving around the lot once, she stopped and threw up her hands in glee and yelled, "I can drive! I can drive! "She looked so sexy. When a woman is happy, she is most beautiful and sexy! I couldn't resist myself and bent over to kiss her and said. "Congratulations!" She pushed me away and said, "You called that a kiss? That's called a peck! Let me show you how to kiss!" So she bent over, cupped my face with her hands and pulled me over to give me a kiss. My goodness, That was a KISS. What a Kiss!

Much later I learned it was called the French kiss. She wrapped her soft full lips around my mouth then slipped her tongue into my mouth. Her tongue literally melt in my mouth and then she sucked my tongue. That's when I realized the mouth is a sexual organ also.

Sex Organs

Speaking of sexual organs, there are a lot of common misconceptions we need to dispel right now. An organ may have different functions.

For example, the mouth is an organ for eating, speaking, sometimes breathing, and also for sex. We usually think of sexual organs as penis and vagina only. But as I just realized the mouth is an important sex organ, also the nipples, and the skin. As I found out later the most important sex organ may well be your brain! I will talk about that later. For now, I want to discuss the differences between male and female sex organs. The penis is actually three organs in one, urinary, reproductive and sexual. Both your urine and semen come out of the same opening, and you derive pleasure from it.

However, in women, the three functions have separate organs. Their urine and babies come out of different openings while they have another organ called the clitoris specifically designed for sex. What men think of as the pussy refers to the birth canal which is actually mainly a reproductive organ. This little anatomical fact is important for men to know, otherwise, they may be missing the "point" literally, when they engage in sex. Being a reproductive organ, nature designed it to have a few nerves endings so that it will be less painful when the baby forces its way out. There are individual differences, some more sensitive than others, but most are insensitive. I met a most extreme case with a woman I managed to have sex with while showering. Afterward, she asked, "Were you inside me?" I was shocked and said, "We did it all that time and you didn't even know if I was inside you?" She said she just wanted to make sure! She later explained that her doctor said her birth canal was fibrous, an unusual condition.

The important thing here is that most men are actually barking up the wrong tree, or should I say, digging the wrong hole. At least they are missing the point. The point is the clitoris which is located on top and outside the vagina. Although it's only peanut-sized, it is the center of women's sexuality, and female orgasm depends on it. A lot of nerve endings are concentrated there similar to the head of the penis. The clitoris is an incredible organ when you think about it. It's an organ without any biological function, it's not necessary for reproduction. Its sole purpose is to give pleasure to women when they engage in sexual activities. In fact, there are more than two billion women in the Middle East and Africa, according to WHO, who are victims of what used to be called female circumcision and now properly called FGM— female genital mutilation. It is an old established custom in those countries to cut out young girls' clitoris so that they become baby machines only, and incapable of enjoying sex. It's a barbaric and cruel crime against women, and I don't understand why there is not a bigger outcry to abolish it.

Clitoris

The clitoris is necessary for orgasm but not necessary for reproduction. I said humans are unique in the animal kingdom in that their sexuality is divorced from reproduction. Actually, that's only true of women but not true of men. In men, their sex is still pretty tied up with reproduction. The climax of men's sexual pleasure, orgasm, coincides with an ejaculation of the semen, which is a reproductive act. Women can get pregnant without clitoris as millions of FGMed women attest. So, why is it there? It is an organ purely for pleasure. It's God's gift to women! It's the apex of evolution. Evolution has finally come up with an organ purely for pleasure. In this respect, women are more evolved being than men. Women are truly human while men are still at the animal level.

Getting back to my Flora. After she showed me what a kiss should be like, she said, "Why don'r you ever date me?" I said. "I thought you were married." She said, "No, not yet. I will be getting married next month, but before that I would really like to get together with you." I said, "I am not doing anything this weekend." She said, "That's great. I will see what I can do."

That Saturday evening, around nine Flora called. She said she was in the neighborhood and she would be over in a few minutes. It turned out her fiancee lived in my neighborhood, a model racially integrated area rare at that time. She seemed to be in a hurry, she said, "I am at my fiancee's birthday party. Since we are running low on beer, I told him I would go and get some more. So, here I am, but I can't stay long." So, I took her up to my bedroom. She undressed quickly and helped me unbutton my trousers.

We hopped in bed and since we had no time for ordinary foreplay, I got on top of her. What a surprise, she was sooo soft, I have never touched any woman so soft before or after! That's probably because she was at the highest state of sexiness. She guided my penis into her vagina and started massaging her clitoris against my penis.

After a while, she decided to roll over so that she would be on top of me and started serious work on me while kept saying, "Oh, that's good, Kuni!" And the thought she really wanted me excited me even more, I was about to explode. I was worried I would ejaculate too fast as I usually do. But to my surprise she suddenly tensed up, held me tight, her body quivered and we both came together! Afterward we held each other tight for a few minutes. It seemed like an eternity.

Heaven could not be better!

She got up to dress and I just stayed in bed to watch her. What a beautiful sight! Have you ever seen the female muscovy duck preening herself after copulation? It's a picture of happiness! She preens her feathers, splashes her wings, and swims around the lake as if it belongs to her. Flora was putting her clothes on with one hand while preening her hair with another, a picture of a satisfied female muscovy duck! She finally put on her lipstick and turned around to look at me with her big eyes and said, "That was so good! Thank you. I must go back. You stay in bed. I'll lock the door," then she was gone. Talk about manhood, for a woman to tell you, "Thank you" after having sex with you, THAT is real manhood!

She was so different from the few other women I had sex with up to that point. It's like they are hard to get, hard to arouse and not really want it and make you feel like they are doing you a favor. Here is someone who really wants you, who actively goes after her need, and who knows what to do. What a change from the majority of women I've met so far. That's the way things should be. That's the way things were before the rise of civilization. But as things are that was a rare occasion for her also, I am sure. She knew she was going into the marriage situation which meant a complete restriction of her sexual activities.

That was the last chance for her to be free. Instinctively a woman knows that marriage is an institution aiming at restricting her sexual freedom.

Marriage

Let's talk about marriage as an institution. It's a fairly recent invention in human history of more than three million years. How did it all begin? It all started with the rise of agriculture about 10,000 years ago, before that humanity lived in a matriarchy, in which the head of a clan was the mother. There is much evidence for this. In one of the oldest books in China called *Shangshu* we find the statement: "Ancient people only knew who their mothers were, but not their fathers." And the Chinese character for "family name" consists of two words—"women" and "birth"—indicating one's family name used to be the name of "the woman who gave birth to you." There is also archaeological evidence for this. Recently I visited Banpo Village, a Neolithic archaeological site located in the Yellow River Valley, east of Xi'an. This twenty-acre site, dated about 6,000 years ago, provides evidence for the existence of early agricultural settlements. I was especially impressed by the fact that women and men were buried in separate areas and that babies were only found buried with women. That could only mean that there was no exclusive pairing up of man and woman as was done later with marriage. Another fact that stood out was that the women's graves had more grave goods than the men's, clearly indicating that women had more possessions while they were alive.

There was no evidence of a male chieftain, but plenty of evidence for female leaders.

Matriarchy was most likely the predominant form of human life before the rise of agriculture and civilization. In matriarchy, humans live in harmony with nature and with each other. Men and women were largely equal, with women's positions being slightly higher. This natural form of human relationship persisted during the early stage of agriculture. Further development of agriculture with its tremendous advance in human productivity and increase in surplus accumulation created class division and gender inequality. Society was divided into those who controlled and enjoyed the surplus value, the ruling class, and those who worked and produced the surplus value, the ruled. Women's position vis-à-vis men fell from a slightly superior position to that of a subjugated one. Both were accomplished by violence, which became the main means of settling all major human conflicts, and remains so to this day.

The agricultural revolution shattered human equality and gender equality by violent means. The strong became rulers and the weak became slaves. The strong conquered more and more land to build kingdoms and empires. They used the slaves they captured and the treasures they robbed to build palaces and tombs for themselves. In their leisure time, they invented better weapons and hired scholars to think up philosophies and religions to justify their ruling position. That's how civilizations were created. What was once public, the land, now becomes private. Men wished to pass on their private property to their own children. But how do you know who are your children? Women don't have that problem, that's men's problem. So, men invented a method of controlling women's sexual life: marriage.

You are not allowed to have sex with anyone else but me. Sex used to be a private affair between a woman and a man.

Now it became a public affair because you need to announce to the world that a certain woman is now your private property and no one else should touch her. This was men's wishful thinking and not easily done, considering how unnatural this was. Naturally, men and women are both polygamous. Genetically it's advantageous for men to spread their seeds as widely as possible for his offsprings to survive. But that is true for women too. It's also advantageous for the survival of her offspring to come from different fathers. This is manifested in the fact both men and women are attracted to different members of the opposite sex at different times and sometimes at the same time.

The common perception now is that men's sexual needs are stronger than women's.

That's very far from the truth. The biological truth is that men are less developed evolution-wise, their sexual climax coincides with ejaculation, which is short and non-repeatable. While women's climax has nothing to do with reproduction and they are longer in duration and repeatable. I am always amazed to see the intensity and length of some women's orgasms. I know mine is nothing compared to their's which made me wish I were a woman!

May

This reminds me of a relationship I might as well tell it now. While I lived in Toronto I knew a Taiwanese friend who lived there also and naturally we got together. We got along really well, as we share the same hometown, same ethnic background, and same left political views. And most important, we share the same cuisine taste. She graduated from a university in Japan before she came to Canada and married a professor from her hometown. She made really good sushis and often brought them when she visited me.

After I got divorced, she came even more often with sushis and other foods. She regarded herself as my elder sister and really took care of me. Her husband was also a technical advisor to a big company and he had to be away for weeks sometimes. Even though she had four children to take care of, they were all going to school. So, whenever she was bored she would come to see me. One thing I really like about her was her total honesty. We would tell each other all kinds of private things we would not tell anybody else. We were best friends.

One day after finishing the sushis she brought I said, "I really love your sushi, but can we have something else next time? Tell you what, I really miss my mother's chicken wine, can you make it? I tried to make it many times but it never tasted quite right." She laughed and said, "That's my specialty. Why did't you tell me before?" You see, chicken wine has a strong sentimental value for me. When I was growing up in Taiwan during the Second World War, we had nothing to eat. The meat was only available on special occasions such as the birth of a baby. It's the ethnic custom of Hakka people that a mother with a newborn child must have chicken wine for one month. Actually, it is a social welfare measure in a poor country to guarantee the health of both the mother and the child. So, I really miss Hakka chicken wine. This is chicken wine and not wine chicken which is another dish. Wine chicken or drunken chicken is easy to make and quite delicious. The emphasis is on the chicken while chicken wine's emphasis is on the wine. Since wine chicken is so easy to make and so delicious, I might as well tell you right now.

You boil a whole chicken in water until done. Take it out and cool it. Put it in a plastic bag or any container with a cover. Pour enough wine to cover the whole chicken. The wine used in China is Shaoxin rice wine, if you cannot get that the best for my taste is medium-dry sherry. Refrigerate it overnight or two, then enjoy it.

Chicken wine is another story. If you miss one little step, it just isn't right. Actually, it's quite easy too, here is May's recipe: You cut the chicken into mouthful pieces, cut up a handful of fresh ginger root, stir fry them with sesame oil (that's the little step I missed) in medium fire until golden brown, pour in half bottle of medium-dry sherry (if you are in China use home-brewed rice wine, Japanese sake is no good), simmer until the meat is cooked, then pour in the other half plus another bottle, increase the fire but watch it closely and turn off the fire just before it boils. You don't want the alcohol to evaporate when it boils.

Remember the emphasis here is the wine. You drink the wine and accompany it with chicken! Don't add salt to it, remember it's chicken WINE.

So, she brought the necessary ingredients and cooked in my kitchen. After twenty-some years I finally tasted my mother's chicken wine again. I had been trying to make it many times but every time something was missing. I like to cook and I enjoy different cuisines from different cultures. Whenever I eat some dish I like I can usually duplicate it myself because I know how it should taste like. Following the recipe from a book is no good as I don't know how the end result should taste like.

The wine chicken case was puzzling for me because I knew how it should taste like but couldn't duplicate it. I thought my taste memory was wrong after all those years. It turned out there was nothing wrong with my memory, I just missed sesame oil! She told me a similar story. She said she always felt the cabbage she had in her childhood in Taiwan tasted so much better than the ones in N. America. Her children said, "Come on, cabbage is cabbage, how could Taiwan cabbage be better. You are just nostalgic that's all." She began to think so herself until she went back one year and found out Taiwan cabbage was really as good as she remembered! Taste memory is incredible and infallible. I had a similar experience with wine tasting. Years ago when I started wine tasting, I got a bottle of Filhot Sauternes, 1983. That was the first time my family had Sauternes, and we were all amazed at how good it was. Since then I had been trying different, more famous Sauternes including the most expensive Chateau d Yquem, but was disappointed. None of them even came close to that bottle of Filhot, 1983. After twenty years we all came to the conclusion it was probably because it was our first Sauternes like first love, you know. But on my 80th birthday, my cousin gave me a bottle of, I don't remember the name, Sauternes. It was incredible, we all agreed, it was as good as the first one!

After the chicken wine dinner, we were both a little tipsy. Luckily she lived in an apartment only a few blocks away and I decided to drive her home. As I stopped in the basement parking garage to drop her off, I bent over to give her a peck to thank her for the delicious chicken wine.

Obviously, the chicken wine was working on her also, a peck was not enough for her.

While I was pulling away she pulled me back to give me a quick kiss then pushed me away. So I straighten back, but she pulled me back again. Push and pull, push and pull went on for a few times. If you know a children's book called Dr. Dolittle, you know a strange animal called Push-me-Pull-you. Well, I've finally met one! She was pushing me and pulling me at the same time, a living example of Freud's Id and Superego wrestling. Her body tells her she wants me but her mind tells her she shouldn't.

This time her body won. She took me to her apartment. She was a few years older than me, in her mid-forties. She was pretty and petite, a head shorter than me, and I am already short at five foot five. But she was well proportioned with long legs and for an Oriental, unusually large bosom. Proportion is very important to me in my esthetic sense. She did something I didn't understand before she got in bed. She went and got a large towel to put on the bed before we got on. I thought that was a special Japanese thing due to her long years in Japan. I ask her why? She giggled and with the little girl's shyness said, "Because I flow a lot, the mattress would soak through if we don't have a thick towel!" We quickly got into the business. Not only was she wet down there, but her whole body was also wet with sweat. She kept bouncing me while giggling, I felt like I was trying to hold down an eel! Before I knew what was happening, she gave out a loud scream and her body shivered. It's important to me in sex that my partner is satisfied, and so I pay attention to when she is about to orgasm and try to co-ordinate.

But she surprised me by coming so quickly. That's no problem, it won't take me long. So I continued pumping, but before I could come, she screamed again even louder!

That's the second orgasm. And the third orgasm followed soon after, even stronger. I couldn't believe it, it's a situation I'd never faced before. I didn't know whether to continue or not. As I was hesitating, she gave one last yell and suddenly went completely limp and motionless. She actually fainted! I didn't know what to do but remembered seeing people slapping the fainted in the movies and slapped her lightly. She woke up and asked what happened? I said, "I think you fainted!" She was really embarrassed, and said. "It must be the chicken wine!" Seeing my penis was still un-pacified, she patted it and said, "Sorry, I will make up for you next time." And she was right about the towel, it was soaking wet, and I met the sexiest little bundle in the world! There were next time and next time, but that's another story.

Women Are More Sexual

My relationship with May wasn't a one-night stand, but I bring it up now to highlight the fact that women are naturally more sexual than men. Man's orgasm is tied to ejaculation, a reproductive act. But women can get pregnant without orgasm. After ejaculation, men's reproductive job is done and you need to wait until your semen builds up again. It's not possible for men to have multiple orgasms in a short time span. In women, however, their orgasm is not necessary for reproduction and they can have multiple orgasms. I knew this in theory before and May was the first woman I encountered who proved it. I haven't seen the highest number a woman is capable of, but I have counted sixteen in one hour. So, what is this strange organ, clitoris for and why do women have orgasms? It's actually quite simple, it's nature's lure for women to engage in sex, a corollary to the pain/pleasure principle. You see, reproduction is a life-threatening event for women. In China, your birthday is called "mother's crisis day", because in the old days every time a woman give birth she was risking her life. My oldest brother was a gynecologist who delivered innumerable babies and he told me, "Mother Nature really doesn't give a damn about women, she doesn't care whether the mother lives or dies after the baby is born." I asked why do you say so?

He said, "You see, most women's birth canal opening is not large enough for the baby's head, so after birth mother's vagina is usually torn and bleeding. Without modern medication, especially antibiotics, a lot of women died." In fact, about half of them died after giving birth before the advent of modern medicine. Women were not stupid, they saw the danger and knew the result of sex was babies and probable death. That's certainly is a major reason for women to be naturally leery of sex.

Given this reality, you need an unusually strong lure for women to do something that's a threat to their lives. Voila, mother nature came up with clitoris and orgasm! That's why it's so strong and irresistible. It's nature's lure and nature's reward.

Vaginal versus Clitoral Orgasm

In the last century, there was a hot debate about vaginal orgasm versus clitoral orgasm. I don't know whether it's settled ever. And there was also a lot of talk about the existence of a G-spot in the vagina.

Both were pitiful male attempts to comfort themselves that maybe they weren't totally barking up the wrong tree all these years.

As I said before vagina is quite insensitive and therefore there is no vaginal orgasm possible. As to the G-spot, that's another vain attempt to put something sensitive in the vagina that's not there. May's vagina was unusually sensitive, she claimed she could feel the squirting of my semen when I ejaculated. I thought if anyone had the G-spot, she should. So, I put my finger inside her, felt around, stopped at one spot, and asked, "Is this the spot?" She said, yes, yes.

Then I tried another spot and asked, is this yet? She said, yes, yes again, and she repeated the same answer with other spots. Well, my logic tells me when every spot is a G-spot, there is no G-spot. She was just sensitive all over that's all. There is another thing about this experience that made me think. Ideally, men and women should try to satisfy each other in their sexual encounters. The most desirable situation is if they orgasm together, but that's very difficult. The most common problem is early ejaculation on the male side. If a man orgasms within three minutes he is considered an early ejaculator and regarded as sexually dysfunctional. However, if a woman orgasmed within three minutes before her male partner like May, that's not only not regarded as a problem but on the contrary, considered sexy. There is obviously a double standard here. The reason is that for various reasons, as things stand, women are hard to orgasm, or not at all. Men are easy to orgasm because they are more animal-like and more direct and honest with their sexuality. When their semen is at a certain level they feel a strong urge to get it off and when they find a willing partner they can't wait to do it. And when they do it they are already about to explode and three minutes of such an intensive in-out thrusting is actually quite long. But normally women have been brought up to be cautious and passive about sex. They also have more considerations about sex, more reasons for sex, not just for pure bodily satisfaction. They are more human in that sense. Sex for its own sake like in the one-night stand is a rare thing for women. They regard their sexuality as an asset to be exchanged for something more important like love, security, and whatnot. Sex for them is a means to an end. You can't imagine what kind of reasons they may have in mind; curiosity, boredom, pity, vengeance, for old times' sake, you name it. I can tell a lot of really strange stories. For now, all I want to say is that if a woman allows herself to be actively seeking the satisfaction of her sexuality for its own sake like in one-night stand situations above she would not need foreplay or more than a few minutes, as shown in May's case.

The Hite report

In 1976 there was an extensive survey on female sexuality done by a feminist called the Hite Report. It was during the time when women discovered their clitoris. The big conclusion was that most married women did not find sexual satisfaction in marriage.

She found that 70% of women do not have orgasms through traditional in-out thrusting intercourse but are able to achieve orgasm easily by masturbation or other direct clitoral stimulation. The report also said that when women masturbate they usually orgasm within three minutes. That's big news, as we were told in all sex manuals for years that women were slow to be aroused and you need patient foreplay and long copulation to satisfy them.

Why then when they masturbate they come so easily? I'll tell you why. When they masturbate, they are in control, they are active and not being acted upon, they do it when they need it and not when someone else needs it. In fact, they are acting just like men do when they need it. A one-night stand is so rare and beautiful precisely because it occurs when both parties happen to be at the right time at the right place. That's the way female/ male relationship should be like, but rarely is it.

Related to this is the feminist complaint that women are treated as sex objects. But sexual desire by its very nature is object-directed. It's an incomplete subject in search of an object, their other half, to complete themselves. Women should become subjects and treat men as their sexual objects also. The problem is that women have hitherto been treated as sexual objects only. And the more important point is that we should not treat each other as sexual objects **only.** We are human beings and should be treated with dignity and respect.

Cynthia

In 1974 I was invited to attend the 25th anniversary of the founding of the People's Republic of China, and one of the events I attended was the big banquet at People's Congress Hall. On our table, we found premier Zhou En-lai's short welcome speech. After a while, he was helped to the head table and someone read his speech for him. We all saw how gaunt and frail he was as he was rumored to have cancer.

After he gestured everyone to start, he was ushered out, and we all gave him a standing ovation since we all knew he came to say goodbye. As it turned out that was his last public appearance, and he died in 1976.

What was most memorable for me was the gorgeous woman with tight blue jeans and long flowing black hair next table. She was wearing a white blouse hugging her full bosom and with the lower parts of the blouse tied in a knot showing her navel.

That was such a rare sight in Beijing during the Cultural Revolution when all women were dressed in drab blue or grey khaki uniforms. I approached her when we were all filing out after the banquet was over and asked her where she was from. She couldn't understand Chinese, so I asked again in English, which was good as no one around could understand what was going on with us. She said she was from Japan and she was accompanying her old uncle on this visit to China. I ask where was she staying and it happened I was staying in the same hotel. As we were leaving the Great Hall, her uncle came over and said he needed to go buy some cigarettes before going back to the hotel. I offered to walk her back to the hotel only a few blocks away.

She said her uncle was an enthusiastic leftist and was only interested in politics while she was not interested in politics at all and was bored to tears. When we got to her room I said, "We are lucky to meet each other and we can have some fun in this drab place!" She smiled and put her arms on my shoulder and said, "That would be nice, I thought this trip would be a total dud." I hugged her and started to kiss her and pulled her to the bed. She said, "No.

no. my uncle will be back soon and he is very strict, but I will give you something quickly to remember me by." So she went to lock the door and came back to unzip my trousers and kneeled down to give my throbbing penis an oral. Oh my god! It all happened so fast, and I never had that done to me before. I was so over-excited that before I knew what was happening, I exploded. She was right, it was over quickly and I always remember her!

When it was over I asked her, "Where did you learned that?" She said, "In Japan mothers teach their daughters how to please men. "What a culture! She then said, "You'd better get going, my uncle will be back soon." She said her name was Cynthia and I told her my name and my room number in another floor and asked her to come over after breakfast tomorrow and left. Sure enough, she showed up after breakfast at about eight but seems to be in a hurry. She said, "I can't stay long. My uncle doesn't know where I am and we are scheduled to leave for the Great Wall at nine." I said, "I am going to the Great Wall too. That's great, maybe we'll meet each other there, but we still have a whole hour to ourselves." So we locked the door and quickly undressed. She was so beautiful! I exclaimed, "You are so gorgeous!" She said, "Don't you think my breasts are too small?" Actually, her breasts are quite large for an Oriental. She was probably thinking since I came from Canada, I like big breasts like most Westerners. And the funny thing is that most Asian women think their breasts are not big enough even when they have larger than usual ones. I said, "No, yours are big enough for me, I actually don't like them too big." Since we were on the topic of breasts I looked closer at hers and said, "Your nipples are really beautiful, most others I have seen are very dark." Her nipples and areola were pinkish and especially attractive to me. As we lied down the first thing I did was to kiss and then suckle her breasts. She moaned softly while I reached one hand down to massage her clitoris. She was very wet and I felt her vagina was unusually soft and fleshy, so I looked down. What a sight, she had the largest vagina I have seen with thick pink lips! It reminds me of her lips on her face which is larger than usual also. Let me tell you a secret, the shape of a women's mouth mirrors the shape of her vagina. Is that why some religions require their women to cover their mouths in public? They probably realize that the mouth is a sex organ and that it's shaped like the vagina. Cynthia's vagina was the most beautiful I had seen so far and I instinctively went down on her and sucked her, something I'd never done before. It was pleasantly salty like eating a big raw oyster. She moaned and pulled my hair and said,"Come inside me quick!" So I did, and we both felt a little relaxed and just held each other tight.

Before we knew it an hour had gone by and someone was knocking on my door and yelled, "Time to get on the bus!" We both put our fingers at our mouths, and I whispered, "Do you want to go to see the the Great Wall?" She said, "Nah, the Great Wall will still be there, we can go some other time." So we kept quiet while my tour guide knocked on my door a few more times and finally said, "Professor Fann is not in his room, we'll go without him." So, we had another three hours to ourselves!

Those three hours were a big lesson for my self-discovery. As I said before, satisfying my partner is important to me as I consider it an important part of my enjoyment of sex. I try to hold off my ejaculation, if possible until I feel she is about to orgasm. Usually, I know when a woman is about to come, as her vagina deep down starts to go into spasm and squeezes your penis. I waited and waited that day but that never happened, but she did scream and held me tight once in a while. I kept on my in/out thrusting, sometimes resting, but never pulled out my penis during those three hours. That was incredible for me as, in my eighteen years of marriage, I considered myself an early ejaculator. I had a hard time lasting more than three minutes, much less three hours! It never occurred to me to even attempt it, but here I did it without even trying. So, what's happening here? Well, what I learned that day was that your body reacts differently to different people. They are psychological reasons. With my wife I didn't feel secure, I felt rejected, I didn't feel wanted, I was nervous and the more I worried the harder was it to hold back my ejaculation. But with Cynthia I felt wanted, I didn't have to prove anything, there were no expectations, no promises, I was relaxed, there was no worry about early ejaculation.

Another good example is one of my best friends. His wife was actually quite pretty but years after their marriage and three children later he started to lose interest in his wife sexually and started to have girlfriends one after another. She confided to me once that her friends told her about her husband's affairs and even had a child with another woman. She said she didn't believe them because she knew as a fact that her husband was totally impotent. She was only curious about what her husband was doing with all these women. That put me in a very difficult position, and could only say, "I have no idea." I couldn't tell her, "I know as a fact he is only impotent with you but a tiger with other women!"

Fake and Real Orgasm

The other thing I learned from that three hours was that a woman may want to have sex with you and enjoy it but do not know how to orgasm. Let me first tell you how to distinguish real from fake orgasms.

Cynthia's screams and holding me tightly were typical things women do when they fake orgasm. Sometimes they squeeze their legs tightly. These are things women can fake but there are three things they cannot fake. They are involuntary bodily reactions not under her control. First, her vagina goes into spasm, it squeezes your penis tightly.

That feeling is unmistakable and sometimes last a long time, up to about ten seconds.

That's women's orgasm, and afterward, there are two more uncontrollable happenings: her body suddenly sweats profusely and her heart jumps like crazy, you cannot miss them.

Cynthia was faking her orgasms. She probably learn it from her mother who didn't know how to orgasm herself either. That, I suspect, was the norm in older times. But she really wanted me as shown by her ready vaginal discharge and her behavior.

So I didn't mind her fake orgasms, and when I finally decide to ejaculate it was almost noon. She said, "Thank you, you turned a most boring trip into a most unforgettable one!" That really made my day!

Too bad I didn't see her after that, otherwise I could have taught her how to orgasm as I did with another woman later. I met her at a Jiaozi party I organized. You see, in the 1980s China started sending students to the West. We leftists in Toronto organized a Canada-China Friendship Association to help new students from China to acclimatize themselves into Canadian life. We organized all kinds of activities and the most important one is the Chinese New Year party. At one of the first organizing committee meetings, we were discussing what to do, especially what to serve. Since we didn't have much money, we need to come up with something good and cheap. I suggested making Jiaozi at the party.

Everyone thought that was a great idea and appointed me to organize it. It was such a good idea that the party grew from about thirty people to about two hundred until 1995 when I left Toronto.

Chinese Dumpling

Let me tell you about Jiaozi. It's a dumpling made of rice wrapping filled with meat and vegetable fillings. That may not sound like anything special, but let me tell you, I taught a course on aesthetics and my conditions for a thing to be really beautiful or delicious are those that are liked by these eight groups of people: man or women, young or old, domestic or foreign, and ancient or present. Well, Jiaozi is such a thing. I lived in N. America for forty years, and whenever I served Jiaozi, I had never met a single person who didn't like it, be they young or old from any county, and most of them never had it before.

So, Here is my recipe: There are ready-made frozen wrappings you can buy from most large supermarkets. The filling is made with half minced pork mixed with the other half consisting of equal parts of finely chopped cabbage, celery, mushrooms, green onion, and a few slices of fresh ginger root grounded. Put in a few tablespoonfuls of soy sauce to taste and mix in an egg to make the mixture stick.

Put a teaspoonful of filling for each wrapper and squeeze it tightly shut. Boil it until done or pan-fry them until golden brown, in which case they are called pan stickers. Oh, don't forget my special sauce everyone always asks for: stir fry some chopped green onions, put in half soy sauce and half vinegar and add some hot pepper if you like it hot. Then enjoy yourself. It's a meal in itself. Also to be noted is that it's something you never get tired of, the only comparable thing may be sex!

So at one of those parties I met this exquisite dish of a woman who strolled in late with very high heels and a short skirt. I usually like long skirts better on women as it makes their legs appear longer and I like long legs. Her legs, however, were naturally long and she was wearing a matching sleeveless blouse showing hairy armpits. I don't know why I find women's armpits hair sexy, remind me of pubic hair? Is that why Western women shave theirs?

Betty

At any rate there she was exuding sexuality and I noticed all eyes were on her like, who is she? Being the host of the party, I walked over to welcome her and showed her where to sit. naturally, I sat next to her and found out she was from Hong Kong. Her name was Betty with a Chinese last name, so I asked, "But you don't look Chinese, you look more like a Polynesian to me." She said, "You are right, my father was Malaysian. "Later I learned that when her mother was young she got pregnant by a Malaysian sailor and gave birth to her but he disappeared after she was born. Her mother finally met up with a wealthy Chinese merchant who married her and settled down in Hong Kong. I also learned she was married to a Chinese martial art instructor and has two teenaged kids. That's bad news as I have my own strict rules about my sexual objects: no married women, no students, no wife's best friend or best friend's wife. But she was my fatal attraction. Not only do I have a soft spot for dark-skinned women like Polynesians, Filipinos, and Indians, but she was also the most beautiful woman I have ever met. Her face was roundish like the full moon, her eyes were large and bright, her face reminded me of tree-ripened peach, and her mouth was like a rosebud about to bloom. I was overwhelmed by her stunning beauty, and when the party was about to be over I asked for her phone number and said I would like to keep in touch as I have things I like to discuss with her. She was working as a clerk in the government. I called her next week while she was working and asked to meet her for lunch near her workplace. She agreed and while lunch was been served she asked me why I wanted to see her. I said I knew she was married and I had no intention of interfering, but I really like her and would be honored to just see her once in a while and would not make any sexual advances. She said. "That's good. What a relief to meet a man who doesn't want sex only. I don't see what's the big deal about sex. When my husband have sex with me I can't wait for him to finish so I can sleep!" So, we agree to be friends, and for the next two three months, we had our luncheon meeting every week. I was surprised I was quite happy with the arrangement especially since she was becoming more and more friendly with me. She started to ask me to take her to Dim Sum, a Hong Kong specialty we both loved.

Dim Sum

"Dim Sum" is the Cantonese pronunciation of two Chinese words meaning "touch" and "heart", best translated into English as "hit the spot". and that truly describes the cuisine. What an invention! The first time I had it was in Hong Kong in 1972 on my first trip to China. I stopped there for a few days to see my philosophy friends.

Every day we met at a Dim Sum restaurant as the city was too crowded and no one had a big enough house to invite guests in, and restaurants were where they socialized.

Consequently, they developed a cuisine to match the social need. The meal consists of various bite-sized food on small plates. Old ladies would wheel their carts stacked with hot food in their bamboo steamers fresh from the kitchen and she would call out what she had: "Har-gao, Siu-mai, Char-siu, I-qi-gao, Fong-jao!" The last one means phoenix claws but is actually chicken feet. It may sound grotesque to Westerners but it was my favorite, and I was amazed how the cook could turn such a lowly thrown away part of chicken into such a delicious bite.

You point to what you want and she would put it on your table. Then other carts would come to your table with different foods. This went on all day from eleven in the morning until late in the evening. And there was always hot tea suppled continuously without charge. In fact the whole experience is also called "Yam Char" meaning "Drink Tea".

What a good way to socialize! I thought this cuisine culture should spread to the world like Japanese Sushi did. Sure enough ten years later Dim Sum places sprung up everywhere in Toronto like bamboo shoots after the rain.

So we started to go to Dim Sum every weekend. At that time I was legally separated from my wife and had a lot of time on my hands and I told her that if there was any function she wanted to attend I would be happy to chaperone her. She said that's great as she didn't like to do things with her husband. I said why did you marry him? She said he was a second-generation Chinese and he had three things all girls from the East wanted: a Green card (residency card), a car and a house. That's when she had just graduated from college and when her student visa was about to expire. "So, I quickly married him after a friend introduced him. I didn't even know him. And he wasn't interested in talking to me like you. He only wanted sex from me and I really don't feel anything when he was doing it and just want him to get it over with as soon as possible," she said. "What a shame!" I said. "You married for the wrong reason. A beautiful woman like you deserve better! You should meet someone you really love. Give me your right hand, I am a good fortune-teller." I kept my promise and never touched her during the first three months but now decided to move on to the next stage by resorting to my old trick.

Fortune Telling

How did I become a fortune-teller? You may wonder. My specialty was palm-reading.

Here is my story. I went abroad after graduating from high school. I had never been close to a girl before I went abroad, let alone touch her. In the first two years after I arrived in America, I couldn't speak English well, so I didn't dare to date. Two years later, my English had improved a little. I started to date an Indian girl from Trinidad, and I thought everything was going fine, but three months later she suddenly dumped me. A few months later, I saw that she had another boyfriend. I plucked up my courage to ask her, why did you dump me? Wasn't everything going well? She said, "It was well, but we'd been going out for three months and you didn't even touch me once. I thought you were gay!" It dawned on me that in dating, men should be quick to make body contact! The trouble was that I was too bound by Chinese feudal ethics. Isn't it sexual harassment to touch someone for no reason? You have to have a reasonable excuse to touch someone!

I finally thought of a good excuse. I went to Chinatown and bought a palm-reading manual. On my next date, within two minutes, I said, "I can read palms!" She holds out her hand at once. I said, "Wrong hand. Man, left hand; woman, right hand", which seemed very learned. With this trick, I solved the "touching" problem, and quickly entered the western world of dating.

And, how did I become a very "good" fortune-teller? First of all, I have taught philosophy all my life, and my greatest self-appointed duty as a teacher is to teach students how to avoid many "scams" they would encounter in their lives. Ghosts, fortune-telling, horoscopes, astrology, Feng shui, religion, etc. are all scams. The common premise for all these scams is to make money, and the way to make money is to exploit the weakness of human nature. Take fortune-telling as an example. First of all, everyone wants to know their future in advance, especially when there are big decisions to make and they are uncertain.

But this is impossible because the future does not exist yet. Then, why do so many people think some fortune-tellers are very accurate? let's start with one of the oldest and most typical fortune-telling stories.

Homer's "Epic" tells the story of a king who wanted to wage war on his neighbor. Of course, he wanted to know whether he would win or not.

He brought a gift and asked the most famous fortune-teller at that time, who calculated and said, "In this war, a big country will be destroyed." The king was overjoyed and immediately attacked the neighboring country. It turned out that he was routed and he went at once to get even with the fortune-teller, saying, "You said I would win, you're a big liar!" The fortune-teller said, "Did I say you would win? What did I say? I said a big country would be destroyed, and you are the big country yourself!" There are several important points in this story. First, a good fortune-teller doesn't say anything that can be wrong. In fact, what he says is mainly nonsense. The reason why the person who has his fortune told thinks the fortune-teller is accurate is that he himself draws his own conclusion. If the king won, of course, he would reward the fortune-teller and say how accurate he was. The point is to say things that are ambiguous, logically infallible, or mostly infallible, or unverifiable right away.

So I took Betty's right hand and read her palm and said, "You like beautiful things (she nodded), you're artistic (nodded again), you're not easy to mess with, if someone wrongs you, you'll hold a grudge for ever (nodded also)......(in a few seconds) Actually you're very generous and will forgive those who have wronged you (nodding strongly), ...This is your lifeline.

Oh, you'll get really sick at 65 or so! But fortunately you'll get through it. You see, you have a long lifeline and will live a long life!......And this is your love line. A lot of people chase you, but you're very picky,.....

It says right here your first marriage is not very happy......This is a great lucky year for you, you'll meet your true love!". She was amazed, she said she had seen many fortune-tellers before and none of them were accurate and I was the only one who could read her mind! I didn't know whether that referred to my last prediction but I certainly planted the seed in her mind. And I told her about some of my experiences with other women. She listened closely and seem curious women could enjoy sex.

Let me digress a little and talk about marriage again before I continue with the story. Marriage like Betty was probably not that uncommon. "Marriage is the graveyard of sex." said some sage. I don't know who said it if no one said it. I say it now. Just think about it clearly. We are naturally polygamous but the traditional marriage is monogamous. That's the most extreme and restrictive sexual arrangement you can imagine! The ideal Christian marriage is this: No sex before, no sex after with anyone else for life! As it turned out for most people, it became no sex for husband and wife also. I never believe in marriage, but one reason I got married the first time was the thought that at least it solved my sexual problem.

But as it turned out it was eighteen years of the sheer desert! I know of many examples, the most tragic example was one of my close friends. On one of his trips back to Taiwan his family introduce a real smart and beautiful girl who had just graduated from a university. They got married without knowing each other well, and soon they had two children. When I visited them and met her for the first time, I sensed something was wrong as she kept complaining about my friend and said finally, "I would divorce him if weren't for the children!" Later I asked him, "She doesn't even like you why are you still married?" He said as long as she still let him have sex with her once in a while he won't consider divorcing her. Well, years later that day came. He said his wife told him one day she wouldn't have sex with him anymore because she had just returned from seeing her elder sister at her death bed dying from cancer, and her sister told her that the only thing she regretted in her life was allowing her husband to have sex with her! And she felt the same way and she didn't want to repeat her sister's mistake.

Oh my God! How should a man feel when you hear that from your wife of twenty-some years? I didn't blame him for becoming a sex maniac in his later life when he could meet women who liked to have sex with him.

Back to Betty and I.

The next weekend she wanted me to accompany her to her friend's birthday party with dancing afterward. On our way to the party, we got into a heated political argument, something I rarely do because I had a very radical leftist view and always got into heated arguments with friends. That's certainly something to be avoided if you want to get into bed with her! But that day Reagan had just invaded Grenada and killed its elected leftist Prime Minister Maurice Bishop. I was upset by the news coming from the car radio and Betty asked what's happening. I told her what I thought and she said she agreed with Reagan and Bishop was a communist, therefore, should be gotten rid of. A democratically elected leader of a nation, and to invade and kill him? I didn't expect my girlfriends to be leftist but a complete political idiot? Politics was very important to me and I almost decided to turn around and forget this beautiful idiot. However, we just arrived at the party and went in but sat through the whole birthday party without saying a word to each other. When the dance music started playing, she got up and took me to the dance floor. Well, she was wearing the traditional Chinese yellow silk Qipao, a body hugging one piece gown with slits all the way up to the waist almost. This should be banned also for being too sexy! There she was, standing there showing all her stuff, sending all men up in the clouds, and I was privileged to hold her in my arms. That was too much!

My anger at her political idiocy evaporated into thin air. I could feel her nipples against my chest, and her body began to get warmer and softer. And this was someone who claimed she didn't like sex? So I said, "This place is pretty boring, you want to leave?" She said O.K. and she agreed to go to my place.

On the way home, I explained to her that she didn't like sex with her husband did not mean she wouldn't like it with someone else. She must have felt something different that day as shown by her body language on the dance floor. When we got to my place, I kissed her and undressed her without any resistance as I expected.

So I quickly put my penis into her vagina without any difficulty as she was very wet. But there was a surprise, her vagina was very tight, unusual for a woman who's had babies. You see, there is a big difference between the vaginas of women who gave birth to babies and those who did not, one is loose while the other is tight. May had four kids and although her body was petite her vagina was very loose. Neither makes any difference to women in sex, as their vaginas are insensitive anyway, and their pleasure comes from the clitoris. But it makes a big difference to men, as a tight vagina is more stimulating to them. Some men are obsessed with the size of their penis, as if the bigger the better for women. That is a common male myth, as I always remind them, firstly the vagina is insensitive, and secondly, no matter how large your penis is, it is not as large as a baby head!

Betty's vagina being unusually tight, I was very stimulated, and knowing she probably wouldn't orgasm, I didn't wait for her and ejaculated quickly. Afterwards I asked her about the special tightness of her vagina.

She said both her babies were born by the Cesarian section and not by natural birth.

That explained why. She started to apologize for not being able to orgasm. I said, "No. no, I was truly happy to just see you, and now I feel really honored that you accept me to do something you don't really like." She said, "No, no, I really enjoyed it. I feel things I never felt before. Maybe you are right, our bodies react differently to different people." So we decided to see each other again and again and again for—-eight years. But that's another story and here I just want to finish this story.

So we dated two-three times a week, first to Dim Sum then to my house or to her apartment which she just rented. She seemed to like the whole process more and more even though she still couldn't orgasm. I was perfectly happy that she seemed to be genuinely enjoying being with me. She asked at one point, "What is orgasm like?" I said, "It's hard to explain. It's like when you sneeze, you go Ah, ah, ah—-Choo! orgasm is the Choo! Or it's like when you blow a balloon, you blow and blow and it finally goes Boom! Don't worry about it. It will come naturally before you know it." And while making love to her a flurry of sweet talk would pour out of my mouth, like "Oh Betty, I love you so much, you are so so beautiful. I thank God or whoever created you, you are the best in the world, ..." and I meant every word of it. I noticed women really like sweet talks, even though they may not really believe it. But I sensed her body was reacting to it since she was more and more excited. One day, after about three months. I was working away at her and sweet talking as usual, and as I was saying, ".... Oh, Betty, I am so excited, please suck me in, I want to get inside you, I want to be your child, I want you to be my mother, ..." Suddenly I felt this vise grip like squeeze on my penis and she screamed and the earth shock and she held on to me so tightly I felt I actually dissolved into her.

That's the unity of Heaven and Earth! It seemed like an eternity, then she let go of me, sat up, looking startled, and asked, "What happened to me?" I said, "You just had an orgasm!" She looked at my limp penis, took it into her hand, and said, "He is so cute! Thank you little Kuni!" and kissed it. From then on we were inseparable. I did not do an actual count but a rough count is something like: we made love more times in one month than I did with my wife in one year!

The Threat of Death and Sexuality

There was another especially unforgettable experience with her which I might as well tell it now. The next year 1984, was the 35th anniversary of the founding of People's Republic of China, and I was invited to visit it for three weeks and take along my spouse or partner. So I asked Betty if she wanted to come with me. She was delighted, but her husband was determined to stop it and convinced her mother and sister to help dissuade her from doing it. So they called a meeting at her apartment and insisted I come to it. That's the kind of situation I was afraid of going out with a married woman!

She said it was O.K. for me to attend the meeting and didn't have to say anything. She didn't say anything either for about thirty minutes and just listened to their reasons against her going. Then she stood up and said. "You are talking about my life, you are trying to decide for me. Have you asked what I want? I want to go! You can all leave now." A woman in love is not to be messed with! I was so proud of her!

So, we went to China and had a fabulous time together traveling as a couple. The most unforgettable episode happened in Tibet. Since I came from a minority ethnic group called Hakka people, I was especially concerned about how minorities were treated in the country. So when the government asked what I wanted to see, I named Tibet as a top priority. Tibet wasn't really ready for visitors at that time. There was no commercial airport, for one thing. We stopped at a military airport and rode on an open truck into Lhasa. There were many memorable things about Tibet and I should probably write a book about what I saw of Tibet about forty years ago, but for now I will tell only one strange event that happened to me sexually. You see Lhasa is about 4000 meters above sea level and the air is very thin. I suffered serious high altitude problem, especially since I found out much later I had a congenital heart problem. Lack of oxygen was actually life-threatening to me. The minute I arrived in Tibet I started to have a splitting headache and vomited every thing in my stomach. I had no energy to walk or even talk. I had no choice but to lie down in my hotel bed. But that first evening a strange thing happened to my body. I felt the strongest sexual urge like I had never felt before or after. That, while I was feeling like dying? Luckily Betty was with me but she didn't think we should do it under the circumstance. Seeing my frenzy, she gave in and cooperated. I exploded the minute I entered her, the quickest ever in my life. I felt better for a while, but another strange thing happened. I got a hard on again in a few minutes and this never happened before either. So I bothered her again and after my second ejaculation, I fainted for a few minutes. After I woke up, I felt much better and could rejoin my tour group again the next day.

This whole experience was so strange that it puzzled me for years until I came up with a reasonable explanation as an old farmer in my retirement. You see, I have a lot of orange and mango trees in my garden.

Sometimes an orange tree would blossom and bear fruits ahead of all others, and I noticed its leaves were yellow and its trunk was attacked by insects. Also when my healthy mango trees won't bear fruit, my neighboring old farmer friend would tell me to give its trunk a few whacks with a machete. So, what's going on here? Being a logician, I started thinking, and not any regular kinds of thinking like Deduction or Induction. I used Abduction. Bet you've never heard of such kind of logic, and I don't blame you. No one else knows it either, because it was invented by a forgotten great American philosopher called Charles Sander Peirce, and I wrote a book on him called. "Peirce"s Theory of Abduction". He thought when we meet a strange phenomenon like I just did, we need a special logic of discovery to come up with a hypothesis to explain it. He first called it Hypothetical Reasoning, then invented a new word Abduction to match the other two well-accepted kinds of reasoning, Deduction, and Induction. People thought the logic of discovery was covered by Induction but that's wrong, for Induction only proves whether a theory is true or not, but to come up with a good theory requires Abduction. A good Abduction comes up with a theory that explains hitherto unexplained facts and the more the better, and it has predictive power. This kind of reasoning is actually widely employed in science, medical diagnosis, detective work, etc.

Abduction

Now I will show you Abduction at work. First, let me name a few other that seem totally unrelated strange facts that are hitherto unexplained. A shrimp farmer told me that when his female shrimps don't lay eggs he catches them and cuts off one of their eyes then they lay eggs. A goldfish farmer told me when his fishes don't seem to reproduce, he drained his pond water to half full then they reproduce. From there we jump to an even more surprising fact. In the American West when criminals were sentenced to death by hanging, people noticed that the hung men would have erections. Now you tell me what all the above strange facts and my orange and mango trees have in common? Well, they all started their reproductive activities when their lives were threatened. So, I used my Abduction and came up with this theory: "When a living being's life is threatened, it switches to the reproductive mode when it is able to." This is a corollary to Darwin's theory of evolution worthy of a Nobel prize! It explains a lot of strange facts and like any scientific theory, has predictive power. It explained my strange behavior in Tibet. A law of nature was working on my body under oxygen deprivation and there was nothing I could do, my life was threatened. It also explains why there are aphrodisiacs for men but not for women. Different cultures have different formulae with strange ingredients, they really work for men because they are all slightly poisonous, not enough to kill you but enough for your body to feel life-threatening. They work on men because men's reproductive act consist in ejaculation of the semen which can be done just before they die. However, these concoctions don't work on women because their reproductive act requires nine months of pregnancy and nature does not waste its time to make women sexy when they are about to die! The last part of my theory, "It switches to reproductive mode when it is able to," is important. When you cut off a male cockroach's head it simply dies, but if you cut off a female cockroach's head as I have done, she would lay eggs if she can. My theory also explains a few other things that used to puzzle me. When I read the biographies of Impressionist artists like Gauguin and Modigliani, I was impressed by their romantic lifestyle. They seemed to me unusually sexual, I thought all artists were like that. Actually, they were all dying from consumption or syphilis. Have you heard of a perverted sexual act some young people engage in nowadays? It's called asphyxiation. As its name implies they actually try to asphyxiate each other with pillows. As my theory predicts it actually works, but you have to know when to stop, for one thing. It's a really dangerous game because you really have to threaten someone's life before he becomes very sexy. For another more important point is that this does not work on women for the reason I just explained. Only I know this, and now you know, but young people who did this didn't know. So, I read in the newspaper, once in a while a woman would die from this kind of game!

Leila

Well, I have digressed, but they are still within the topic of sex. Back to the one-night stand. I taught at a college for many years.

Everyone in the college recognized the most beautiful woman was the secretary of the college council, Leila. She was always dressed in name-brand fashion, tastefully made up, and wore Chanel 5. She was a picture of prim and proper! She ran the college council like clockwork, she was a picture of efficiency! She rarely smiled and never chit-chatted with anyone, only college business. It was totally not within my imagination to picture her as a possible sex object. But the impossible happened. We in the college always held a year-end Christmas party. We ate, drank and danced as usual and at the end of the party I noticed she had quite a bit of alcohol, as her face was unusually red and her steps were not steady. I said, "You shouldn't drive home yourself. You should have someone else drive you home." She said, "You are right, I shouldn't drive. Would you drive me home?" Of course, I said yes. Then she said she needed to go to her office first to get her stuff before going home, so I followed her.

When we both got into her office, she turned around to shut the door and in the process, her high heel caught the thick rug on the floor and she stumbled. I quickly caught her in my arms and suddenly smelled her alcoholic breath and warm soft body. I don't remember who was kissing who first but we ended up on the rug and started undressing each other. After we were both naked she ran her hands through my torso and said, "You have no body hair, I've never been with a Chinese, you feel so silky, that's kind of nice." I asked, "What kind of men have you been with, and what were they like?"

She said, "They were mostly Jewish and they were all hairy chested." I said, "Are you Jewish? You don't look it, you have blond hair and most of my Jewish friends have dark hair." She said, "That's dyed, look at my pubic hair." So I did, and it was very dark and thick. I could't understand why men used to call women's vagina "pussy", now I know, it reminded them of pussy cat! I like vaginas in their natural state. It's nature's design for men and women to rub against each other comfortably. I don't understand why a lot on women now shave their pubic hair and arm pits hair. And if they are not shaved for a day or two, they feel like sand paper! So, we got down to business, she was like any woman in heat, vagina wet, body warm and soft. I was on top of her plowing away, diligently tilling my piece of land, so to speak. The most memorable of this episode was that afterwards my elbows were bruised. I said, what happened? She said, "That's rug burn!" I'd just learned a new word! So, I was thinking, this has happened before with someone else? And she said, "Oh, that was so good, it's being such a long time!" "How long?" I asked. She said, "Since last Christmas!" My goodness, here was this goddess, coming down from her pedestal, to become an ordinary mortal one night a year, and I was lucky to be in the right place at the right time to receive her favor! I was her once-a-year one-night stand!

To be serious, this is really a shame. Here was a perfectly beautiful and sexy woman, who put herself on a pedestal and lived 99% of a year a social life that's prim and proper, and only allowed herself to be natural for one night with the help of alcohol. I am sure this was an extreme case, but I suspect the attitude toward sex is shared by a lot of women. I went to her office to thank her next Monday, but instead of thanking me back, she was really embarrassed and kept saying she didn't remember what she did as she was very drunk. Obviously she thought she did something wrong and shameful. People in the rest of the world look at N. America as the land of sexual liberation, where people are free to enjoy their sexuality. But I lived in N. America for forty years and I know better.

Even the outwardly so-called liberated women have guilt feeling towards sex unconsciously. Where did this deep seated guilt feeling towards sex came from? I, being a philosopher, pondered over this for a long time and here is one source of the problem.

Ordinary Language Analysis

I will employ a philosophical method inspired by Wittgenstein, popular last century, called Ordinary Language analysis. We believed that ordinary language reveals a lot more about our deep beliefs than a lot of abstract analysis. Here I will show you how the method is put to use. First, I ask myself what are the most common curse words? In English it is probably, "Fuck you!" And in Chinese it definitely is, "Ta Ma de!" Which, literally translated means, "His Mather's!" But his mother's what? And why is it a curse? This was actually an abbreviation for an old Hakka curse, "Fuck your mother's old pussy!" A similar bad curse in English is, "Mother fucker!" Now, why different cultures use the sexual act as a curse? Because, our deep down conception of "fucking" is an bad, dirty, shameful act. Therefore doing that to you or your mother is doing the worst possible thing you can imagine. That's how bad our conception of sex is. There is another important thing to be noted about this kind of curse, The object of the curse is a woman. Even when you are cursing a man you are treating him as a woman in this case. In traditional grammar in the sentence, "X fucks Y", the subject is always a man and the object is a woman. It connotes a man doing something bad to a woman. Women are the victims of "fucking" as things stand, and they unconsciously sense that. That's probably why all women I met disliked the word and preferred the euphemism "love making".

"Fucking" versus "Love Making"

This inevitably leads me to a discussion of "Fucking versus Love Making". This capsulizes the differences between male and female conceptions of sex. Remember my earlier quotation about what Woody Allen's girl friend said? She said. "Sex without love is really an empty experience!" There you have it, a typical woman's conception of sex as something meaningful only with love. That reminds me of people who likes to drink coffee only with cream and sugar. You see, if you like coffee, you don't need cream and sugar, you drink it straight. If you must have cream and sugar to drink coffee, you probably find black coffee too bitter by itself and needs to cover it with cream and sugar. You are like sugarcoating a bitter pill, you don't really like coffee! These women regard sex as a bitter pill to be taken when necessary, but preferably sugarcoated. They regard sex as a means to an end, with the end being love. But what is love? And What do women want? The most important qualities women want in man are reliability and responsibility. What for? To put it bluntly, what she really wants is a meal ticket. You see, in the old days when women's position was very low, her livelihood and her children's depended on the man she marry. Economic consideration was utmost on her mind and no-one can blame her for that. But the century old social reality left an indelible mark in her subconscious mind which even after social reality has changed it remains alive, and surfaces in her conception of sex now. I call this kind of conception as Prostitution Complex, as she considers her sex as an asset to be used in exchange for something she wants, be it money or love. Wasn't it the great philosopher Marx who said marriage was worse than prostitution? For a prostitute is like a free agent who sells her wares piece meal, but a wife sells her sex for life. The later is a form of slavery!

On the other hand, men like to "fuck"

women, because in "fucking" a man is the subject. He is in control. But "fuck" connotes doing something bad. If a man says, in a business transaction, "I am fucked!" or "I am screwed!" You know he means he's been had or cheated. "Fucking" connotes aggression towards women, and when it's pushed to the extreme it becomes rape. Is that why every pornographic film there is a rape scene? Men are excited by such scenes. I call this kind of conception of sex as Rape Complex. Men are more honest in what they want from women, they want sex. But what is wrong is the kind of sex they want. They treat women as sex objects only. They enjoy the aggressive part, they like women to be passive receivers of their aggression. Ideally, sex should be a mutually enjoyable activity between equals. There is nothing wrong with treating each other as sex objects, as that is the nature of sex. Both males and females are incomplete beings seeking each other to complete themselves. The trouble so far is that they are missing each other, one doing it for the wrong reason while the other doing it the wrong way. The way we talk about it reveals our deep misconceptions. In Hakka culture there was a tradition of women as the head of the family, and hence women's position in their community were much higher. This is reflected in the way they talk about sex.

Copulation in Hakka is "Xion Diao" meaning "mutual fuck". That's the way it should be. If and when women can use "fuck" as readily as men do now, and when it has no bad connotations, we have a sure sign we have achieved true sexual equality and liberation.

Christianity and Sex

Before I get into Hakka people, let me go into another source of our general bad attitude towards sex: It's religion. In my high school days, my best friend was a Christian. His father was a pastor of a church. I was very curious about religion in general and Christianity in particular in my youth and visited them often to find out more. A central Christian doctrine says that all humans are born with sin, and need to believe in Jesus to be saved. I couldn't understand why children are born with sin when they haven't done anything yet. They said their first ancestors Adam and Eve disobeyed God by eating the fruit from the forbidden tree. I wondered what was the fruit? They thought it was an apple. What's so sinful about eating an apple? It didn't make any sense to me. They also said Jesus' mother Mary was a virgin, and she remained a virgin all her life, which was incredible to me. So when I went to a Christian college in the U.S., I was determined to find out what was the story all about. I attended the chapel services every Sunday and read the Bible again and again. The story runs something like this: God first made a man called Adam then made a woman called Eve from his rib to keep him company. He put them in charge of the Garden of Eden and told them, they could eat any fruit from the garden but not the fruit of the tree of knowledge of good and evil.

Then the Devil showed up in the form of a big serpent, and tempted Eve to eat the fruit of the forbidden tree, and shared it with Adam. When God found out, he cursed the serpent and said to Eve, "I will make your pains in childbearing very severe; with painful labor, you will give birth to children.

Your desire will be for your husband, and he will rule over you."

This account still doesn't tell me what all the fuss was about. It's still not clear what was the terrible sin that deserves such severe punishment. The key to understanding this story hinges on what was the forbidden fruit. Western tradition says it's the apple, but others say it's either fig or a pomegranate. I think it has nothing to do with any fruit.

Reading from a non-believer's perspective and cutting through a lot of religious gobbledygook, "eating the fruit from the tree of knowledge" is actually a religious euphemism for the sex act. "Know" is used in the Bible as what comes to be generally accepted as "know-someone-in-the-biblical-sense", such as this line in King James Bible, "And Adam knew Eve his wife; and she conceived," or, "When Joseph woke from sleep, he did as the angel of the Lord commanded him: he took his wife, but knew her not until she had given birth to a son." Eve was tempted by the serpent (We don't need a Freud to tell us it's a phallic symbol) to have sex with Adam. So the original sin was sex, and it was all Eve's fault! This is a terrible story. God is supposed to be perfect, all-powerful, all-knowing, and all-loving.

He first made a man and then a woman, both are physically imperfect and psychologically desirous of each other sexually, and He forbid them to have sex? This was a set-up, an entrapment! He set up a trap knowing they would fall for it and then punish them for eternity! What kind of game is this? It sounds more like a sadists' game. If anyone is guilty in this story, it's the entrapper and not the entrapped.

As to the virginity of Mary, the English translation of "virgin" in Hebrew meant more like "maiden", a girl of marriageable age, and nothing about virginity. After Joseph got engaged with Mary he found out she was already pregnant and naturally he was upset and wanted to break off the engagement. "But God soon sent another angel, this time to Joseph, in a dream. The angel reassured Joseph that his marriage to Mary and the birth of this child were His will. Joseph awoke from his dream and took Mary as his wife soon after, ready and willing to raise the child despite the public humiliation he may experience." Joseph, being a religiously properly brought up young man believed in his dream and married Mary. It turned out to be a good marriage for him as she bored him with four sons and some girls. Both stories showed women to be more active with sex, Eve initiated sex with Adam, and Mary got pregnant before she married Joseph. Be that as it may, the conception of sex is that it's something bad and sinful. They could not accept their religious leader to be a product of such a dirty act hence they came up with the virgin birth story.

Buddhism has a similar story. They also consider sex to be dirty and bad, hence they concocted a ridiculous story that Buddha was conceived one night when his mother dreamed a white elephant entered her body. And of course, their religious leader could not be born from such a dirty and lowly place as the vagina, so he was born from her underarm! Why are all religions so anti-sex and anti-women? This is certainly an issue needing an in-depth study. For now, I only wish to point out that centuries and centuries of indoctrination upon billions and billions of people from their childhood has formed our deep-seated conception of sex as bad and sinful.

Hakka people

Back to the Hakka people, let me tell you a bit about their culture and how that's related to their conception of sex. The overwhelming majority of Chinese belong to the Han race. The Hakka are a small minority ethnic group of Han people. They do not constitute a race. But they have a unique language, custom, music, etc. of their own because centuries ago there were waves of refugees from central China due to dynastic changes or foreign invasions. They settled in the southern mountainous part of China, intermingled with the natives, and formed their own identity. They were known as the guest people, which is what "Hakka" means. Because of the harsh condition of life in the poor mountainous region, they are known as hard-working, self-reliant, stubborn, and rebellious people. During one period of their exile life, the central government would periodically come to the area to capture young men for the army. To avoid that, women hid their men indoors, and they worked in the field to show there were no men around. After a while, the roles of the traditional man/woman relationship became reversed in most Hakka families. Man stay home and took care of the children. and cooked meals while women took over men's work outside. Consequently, Hakka women were famous for being strong, independent, and self-reliant.

This is also reflected in their sexual attitude.

They are more active and assertive. May was an example. At one point she ran a donut shop and she had a double bed in the back room of her shop. She would call me whenever she wanted sex, and that was very often. I thought I was a sex maniac but I met my match in her. She was the living example of women's sexual superiority over men. She seemed to need it all the time and had the ability to do so, but I needed a day or two to replenish after each ejaculation.

Usually, I have more sexual needs than my girlfriends, but this time I must admit I couldn't fully satisfy her. She would call me sometimes in the middle of the night, and I was too tired to hop over to her place.

Something strange would happen. She started to talk funny and sound funny and made strange noises. Then I realized she was masturbating over the phone, using me as her sex object! I was her fatal attraction. She confided that she really loved sex, and needed it all the time. Even when she was nursing her baby, she felt sexy and use her baby's toe to masturbate her clitoris.

Sometimes she would go to the swimming pool and find where water comes into the pool, and orgasm quickly from the warm jet of water aimed at her clitoris.

All my life I felt I didn't have enough sex, but this period with May was an exception. I had more than enough. I started to think about the appropriate quantity of sex. In Chinese, the character for "semen" is the same as for "essence". Chinese believe that the semen represents men's essence, their vital energy. Every expenditure of your vital energy is a drain on your energy reservoir.

They point to the average short life span of past emperors as examples since they all had hundreds of concubines.

So they recommend moderation in sexual activities for men. A corollary of his theory is that women as receivers of this vital energy are the benefactors of this transaction. Hence there are a lot of stories about women who knew how to suck men's essence to become more beautiful and long-lived. The Western view is quite different. The sperm is just a few drops of protein. Its expenditure doesn't constitute any significant loss of energy.

Besides, a man cannot have too much sex as you simply cannot do it anymore when your semen is spent.

Nature versus nurture argument

This is really interesting. East and West have totally different theories about some ordinary life issues and I am not sure which is correct. There is another one that always puzzles me. In China, we were told from childhood that if you put your book too close to your eyes or sit too close to watch TV. you will become nearsighted. They even teach children to message their eyes to avoid nearsightedness. But in the West, nearsightedness is considered inherited, there's nothing you can do. Kids put their books close to their eyes because they are already nearsighted! Even my Harvard Medical Encyclopedia says so. Not debatable! Now, which is the truth? I don't really know. Someone should do research on it. But judging by Abduction, we can decide which is a better theory on logical grounds. Pierce said one theory is better than another if it explains more, predicts more, and is simpler. I like to add one more condition, one theory is better than the other if it does no harm and benefits more.

China's theory is better because adopting it does no harm. Massaging your eyes can only benefit your eyes' health, and if some cases of nearsightedness can thereby be avoided, that would be of great benefit. The western theory simply says there's nothing you can do. This theory can do great harm if it turns out there is something you can do.

We come across heredity theory very often in different fields. For example in the nature versus nurture debate with regard to human nature. As things are now, humans are aggressive.

Why? One theory says humans have always been aggressive, that's their nature, there's nothing you can do about it. The nurture theory says it's because of their upbringing, and proper education can change that. Translated into the political arena, conservatives like the nature theory or what I call the "Do nothing" theory.

Progressives like the nurture theory as they believe the status quo can be changed. For the reason I gave above, I am on the nurture side. A similar argument is given about the male/female relationship. We see men and women are unequal in the present world. Why? The conservative view says, that's human nature, It has always been like that in human history, and that's even true in the whole animal kingdom.

This is not only a do-nothing theory but a wet blanket theory.

If it's true then why bother to try to fight for equality? Its purpose is to dampen the struggle for gender equality.

Let's look at the argument. First, is it true the female is inferior in the whole animal kingdom? Anyone with any knowledge of animals knows this to be utterly ridiculous. The animal kingdom is so diverse, there are all kinds of arrangements. Just to give you a counter-example from my farm. I specialize in breeding Eclectus parrots. They are very special in that they are an example of extreme sexual dimorphism, one sex is all green and the other all burgundy red. I have a lot of fun asking all my B&B guests the same question, "Tell me which do you think is the male which female?" Invariably I get the answer, the red one is male and the green one female. Well, actually it's the opposite. There go your stereotypical conceptions about males and females! Not only that, female Eclectus is more aggressive than the male. I often find the male being killed by the female when she is in a breeding mood and he is not cooperating! I'll give you another example from my farm. In the summer I see a lot of giant woods spider in my garden. The female is about 5cm while the male is 0.5cm, only one-tenth of the female's size.

He must be very careful to approach her for mating and runs as quickly as possible after copulation since she regards him as a small snack and eats him when she can!

The argument from nature is based on total ignorance of nature. How about the argument from human history? Is it true that women have always been inferior in human history? This is also based on the total ignorance of human history. As I showed earlier in this book, humans lived for hundreds of millions of years in a matriarchy, and women were suppressed for only about 10,000 years, a brief time in human history. And we are now living in the midst of the transition to gender equality and sexual equality will be an integral part of that transition.

Prostitution

Back to the theme of a one-night stand, I once had a most unforgettable one-night stand with a prostitute. On one of my trips back to Taiwan, a good friend took me to a restaurant for supper. After supper, he said," It's still early, let's go find a place to get a few drinks before we call it a day." So, I followed him to a place and sat down in a cubicle and there was a big dance floor in the middle. I asked, "What kind of place is this?" He said, "In a while different girls will come to offer you drinks, and if you like one you can ask her to sit down and buy her a drink, and she will be your host tonight. After drinking and dancing, if you like her you can take her to your hotel." Then I realized that I was in a night store where you pick up a prostitute. Just then two girls came by, one of them sat down with my friend as she seemed to know him. The other said, "I am May, can I sit with you?" I said, "Yes, but to be honest with you, I was tricked into coming to a place like this. I have done this kind of things before once, and I swore never to do it again. So, don't waste your time on me, I won't take you out later." She smiled and said, "That's O.K. I will keep you company anyway." So we just talked about each other, and when she found out we came from the same village she really opened up and told me a lot of things I didn't know. For example, I remember from my first meeting with prostitutes, they allow you to do anything but they do not kiss. I ask why? She said they consider kissing more intimate than sex, and that they want to reserve that for their husbands if they ever marry.

She asked me if I wanted to dance. I said I was a poor dancer. She said she would show me how and took me to the floor. She was wearing a pink Qipao with the usual high slits and I swear she was like Julia, no bra, no underwear. I thought that was too much and I didn't want her to lure me into doing anything against my principles. So I got off the dance floor and told her I wanted to go home and prepare as I was going back to Canada the day after. So we exchange our phone numbers and promised to keep in touch.

About noontime next day she called and said she was free that afternoon and did I want to see her. I said, of course, got her address, and hopped onto a taxi to go there. When I arrived at the address, she was already waiting on the sidewalk and took me through the first-floor convenience store up to the second floor where she lived. In the middle of the room, there was a Japanese-style wooden bathtub big enough for two and filled with hot water steam. She said, "This winter is kind of cold and I have the hot tub ready for you." I said, "That's really considerate of you, whoever marries you will be a lucky guy." We both undressed and got into the tub and she said, "I hope I meet someone as nice and honest as you in the future." I almost cried and at the same time felt this terrible urge to get into her as quickly as possible. So we got out, dried up, and moved to the Tatami room. We were both very warm from the bath and though the air was a bit chilly we didn't need any blankets. I got into her quickly and she seemed to like it, but something strange soon happened. Her body suddenly became frigid, freezing cold! I soon lost interest to continue for that reminded me of my first experience with prostitutes.

So what happened in my first experience? Years ago, on one of my first visits to Taiwan, I had been without sex for a while and was also curious about Oriental women. So, I booked in a hotel and asked the hotel manager to send me a girl. He said they don't do such a service. I said then I will check out. He then said, wait in your room and we will send one in a few minutes. Sure enough, a short girl showed up. She kind of methodically undressed and gestured me to do the same and bent down to do me an oral. She was pleasant-looking and her body have all the womanly parts, but seemed to me not quite mature. When I tried to get into her, her vagina was bone dry and I had to lubricate my penis with my saliva. When I did get in, her whole body suddenly turned freezing cold. For some reason I quickly ejaculated, but I wouldn't call it orgasm. That was such a grotesque experience I swore right then and there I would never do that again.

As I was getting dressed and telling May I had to go to a wedding reception soon, I thought I should give her some money and handed her a few hundred dollar bills. I said you need the money. but no matter how I tried, she refused to accept, and said, "You are insulting me. That's my gift to you so that you will remember me!" I am glad she didn't take the money from me. if she did she would be just another nameless prostitute. As it happened, it was: "A prostitute having sex with you but refused to take money from you!" That's something to write home about! What an ego booster.

However, as a sexual encounter that wasn't a good example of a one-night stand, since the reason on her part was wrong. She was giving sex as a gift to me and not for its own sake. As you will see in my later examples. women engage in sex for strange reasons and rarely purely for enjoyment as in a real one-night stand situation. That's why I place such high value on it. In the first prostitute's case, I understand why her body froze, as what she wanted was money and definitely not sex, and her body naturally reacted in rejection. Soft and warm mean welcome, rigid and frigid mean rejection. That's the body's natural language. I was puzzled by May's body reaction since she didn't want money and just wanted to be nice to me.

On the other hand, her body's reaction is quite understandable. Your body does not listen to you. it has a will of its own. Her body was used to the frigid reaction wherever a penis entered her. It became a habitual, automatic reaction, not under her control.

Prostitution is a real tragedy in male/female relationships. It turns what should have been a most natural, mutually enjoyable encounter into a meat market transaction. On the male side, it's the most undignified thing a man can do. If you need to pay money to buy fake sex, you are in fact admitting to yourself that I am so unlikable I am unable to find anyone who wants to have sex with me. In that case, all I can say is that It's much better to masturbate, at least you are doing it with someone who likes you! As for women, it's a real tragedy that they have to sell their bodies to make money. Sugarcoating it by calling them "sex workers" is not going to change the nature of the profession. In the process, they sacrifice their sexuality, ruin their ability to enjoy sex. This unique Nature's (or God's) gift to humanity, the ability to enjoy sex for its own sake (beyond reproduction), is defiled in prostitution.

It's easier to see what's wrong with prostitution. It's harder to see traditional marriage is even worse. Just think about what each side is looking for in a marriage. A man is looking for someone beautiful, younger, shorter, weaker, less educated, etc. The first condition is OK, he's been honest, he is looking for a sex object. But the other conditions can be summarized in one sentence, he wants someone he can control. A woman wants a husband who is rich, tall, strong, older, smarter, dependable, etc. They are all conditions for a good meal ticket. Sexual satisfaction is not on the list. They are missing each other even before they are married. No wonder Hite reported 70% dissatisfaction in married women's sex life. And no wonder some women found it regrettable at the end of their lives that they had to put up with their husband's sexual advances. Unlike food where something is better than nothing, sex unless it's good, it's better not to have it. You see, sex is an intimate union of two bodies and minds that when it's good, it's Heaven; but when it's bad, it's Hell. It's a most delicate undertaking. Everything has to be perfect: for the right reason, at the right time, in the right atmosphere, etc. etc.

A Failed One-night Stand

This reminds me of an unsuccessful one-night stand. On one of my trips back to Taiwan, I went to a restaurant with my friends as usual. This time there was this pretty waitress Miss. Chen. I don't remember her given name, as she didn't have an English name. She was tall for a Chinese woman, had all the curves in proper places, and walks in a most graceful fashion. What's more important was her friendliness and ready smile. I asked if she would show me around Taipei before I went back to Canada in a few days. She readily agreed and said she was available next Saturday. So, after meeting her for lunch at a restaurant, she took me to a riverside park that had just opened. We start at a bench looking over the river with a gentle breeze blowing from the river. I said," you are a really beautiful girl, you must have a lot of boys chasing you. Do you have a boy friend?" She said,"Yes and no." I asked."What do you mean?" She said,"I have been going out with this boy I really like for three years, but he hasn't touched me once." I just laughed, and said,"What a fool, just like me when I was younger," and told her about my first girlfriend. "But she dumped me after three months, and you haven't dump him after three years? Why don't you start first and hold his hands next time?" I asked, and held her hands. she said," Girls don't do that." "I don't suppose he kissed you either! Let me give you a kiss for him!" and I bent over to kiss her. She was surprisingly accommodating. She was treating me like an elder brother or she was like a ripe fruit ready to be plucked. So, I said," This is too public, let's go to my hotel. There's more privacy." She readily agreed and we went to my hotel. By that time I was like a volcano about to explode. The minute we got inside my room, I started to kiss her and undress her. Her body was soft and limp, a sure sign she was ready too. I put her on the bed and undressed. As I lay down next to her, I first noticed her black naval. She didn't know how to clean her naval! What's worse, I smelled a stench of rotting fish coming from her vagina! What a killer! My raging fire was instantly extinguished. I quickly got up and said," We really shouldn't do this, you should save this for your boy friend."

Body Order

So, that was my first failed one-night stand. Thinking back, there were as many failed ones and not quite successful ones as really successful ones. But before I go into those, I must tell you what I know about body order. It's not a topic people talk about openly, but it's so important to a sex life that I should go into some details. I have done some research on this topic, so I would like to share my findings with you here. Let me start with bad breath, which is the most common problem and the most troublesome because it is close to the nose and the sense of smell is strange, it quickly adapts to odor, so you won't smell bad breath, and others are embarrassed to tell you. You need to ask a very close person to tell you honestly.

Once, a good friend who often visits me came to see me. As soon as I saw her, I smelled her bad breath. Before she left, I took her aside and told her that you have a strong smell today, do you have cavities?

You need to see the dentist. Instead of thanking me, she stopped coming to see me for years. Bad breath has a great influence on your life, especially your sexual life. I remember that Russell, the great philosopher of the last century, said in his autobiography that his favorite long-term girlfriend dumped him for no reason. Later, he learned that it was because of his bad breath caused by his periodontal disease.

So periodontal disease, tooth decay, sinusitis, tonsillitis, acid reflux, etc. can all cause bad breath, but the most common reason for bad breath is that the teeth are not washed properly, and it is not easy to wash your teeth clean. Just think about it, your mouth is wet and warm, and there is a little bit of food, especially meat, between the teeth, by tomorrow morning it will rot and smell. Traditionally we brush our teeth after getting up in the morning, which is totally wrong. The most important thing is to clean your teeth before you go to bed, otherwise, the food between your teeth will smell overnight. If you brush your teeth clean before going to bed, and your mouth is still clean when you get up in the morning, why wash again? The point is to clean your teeth after every meal.

Cleaning teeth is a tricky business, and brushing teeth is out of fashion. First of all, don't ever use an electric toothbrush, its force is too strong. If you use it for a long time, it will damage your teeth, and ordinary toothbrushes don't quite help. No matter how you brush your teeth, there is still food stuck between your teeth. You must use dental floss to get the food out, which is great progress, but it is not enough yet. If you don't believe me, just go buy a water pick to wash again, you will see that there is still food coming out. Now I only use the water pick, wash the teeth before I go to bed, and gargle after meals during the day, then your teeth will be fine. I strongly recommend you to buy a water pick, which is easy to use, fast, and won't hurt your teeth. I especially recommend it to the elderly, because their own cleaning ability has deteriorated, which causes their problem of so-called elderly smell.

Next, let's talk about the underarms' odor. This odor is very special. It has a strong foxy smell to it. It comes from special glands under two armpits. It is different from ordinary sweat glands. It discharges yellowish sweat when you are nervous. Its smell and function are the same as those of the odor of skunks. I believe this is a special function leftover by human beings from ancient times, with the purpose to prevent beasts from eating you. Some people still have this kind of gland, some people don't.

Some races, like whites and blacks, have more, while the yellow race has fewer, but it has existed since ancient times. History records that during the Spring and Autumn Period, King Chen, a lover of the famous beauty Xiaji had the problem of foxy odor. When I was young, I used to have a smell when I was nervous. Fortunately, I knew that I could buy deodorant in the drugstore and put it on every time after taking a bath.

Later, I was not so nervous and stopped having this problem. Recently, I ran into this problem again. My Indonesian migrant worker is very nice but has a foxy smell.

She took care of me close by, but her smell was really unbearable. After a few days, I finally told her, bought her the deodorant, and solved the problem.

Let me move on to smelly fart. When I was young, I grew up in the countryside, and the sanitary conditions were not good.

Everyone farted and we thought it was natural, and wouldn't feel too bad about it as the countryside was spacious. However, it became a big problem after I went to America. At that time, I had two most troublesome physical problems, one was a smelly fart, other dandruff. I didn't know how to deal with them and was too embarrassed to ask the doctor. Finally, my doctor brother came to America and I asked him for help, but he said we doctors only studied the major life-threatening diseases, and no one studied these small problems. In the end, I solved both problems by myself. I'll talk about first how to solve, by accident, the problem of smelly farts. In 1976, I went to Australia as a visiting professor via Fiji Island. When I got off the plane to rest, the waiter gave me pineapple juice and I began to vomit as I boarded the plane again. As soon as I got off the plane, I rushed to the hospital. I had diarrhea for two days. The doctor told me I was infected with Amoeba from drinking unclean juice, and he gave me a medicine called Flagyl, and I was completely all right in two days. Not only did my stomachache get better, but I noticed that my fart was no longer smelly. It was this medicine that killed all the bacteria that made the smelly fart!

Later, when I went back to visit Taiwan, I smelled my eldest brother's smelly fart. I said you are a doctor, why don't you take some medicine to treat it? He said, Is there a medicine for it, what is it called?. I said, it is called Flagyl, and he said, oh, it's FLA-GI-LU (pronounced in Japanese way), I give this medicine to my patients every day. It turned out that he was an obstetrician and used it to cure Trichomoniasis, a sexually transmitted disease. Men have fewer symptoms, while women's genitals will smell like rotten meat. Only when both of them take the medicine at the same time can the disease be eradicated. If the woman's genital stinks again after eradication, either the man or the woman must be having an affair. The genital smell is the biggest killer in sexual life. Remember this odor-specific medicine, Flagyl, which can be bought in ordinary drugstores without a doctor's prescription. It can not only cure genital bad odor, smelly fart, dentists also use it to treat severe bad breath.

Another Failed One-night Stand

At my university, there was an interdisciplinary study called East Asian Studies, and we would have a get-together party every year. Everyone interested in East Asia would come. At one of these parties, I met this gorgeous woman in her twenties who stood out clearly in the crowd by her self-assured demeanor. Naturally, there were a lot of men gathered around her. For some reason, she decided to sit next to me after we picked our food from the buffet table. We started talking and I found her unusually well-versed in Chinese culture. Her name was Carol with a very British last name. When the party was coming to an end, she said," We should continue our conversation." Of course, I said, OK and exchanged our phone numbers.

The weekend after, I invited her to my house. During our discussion at the party, she expressed interest in the Chinese tea ceremony. So, I set up my tea ceremony wares in my little tea room next to my living room. Surprising for a young westerner, she was quite well versed in Chinese tea ceremonies. The only thing she was not familiar with was the gourd-shaped pottery tea toaster I made for my tea ceremony. So I told her the story about how it saved me from an embarrassment in Moscow. You see, there was a Moscow International Trade exhibition about 20 years ago with the theme of tea. I was asked by the government to represent Taiwan in the trade show to advertise Taiwanese tea. I brought ten pounds of the best tea and one pound of regular tea for comparison. We had a tent on the exhibition ground in the red square.

On an opening day, the organizer of the exhibition arranged for important people to taste my tea, such as the minister of agriculture, the foreign minister, and the owners of the biggest tea houses in Moscow. As they were only familiar with teas from mainland China, and this was their first experience with Taiwan tea, I started by explaining the differences. I said," Tea makers in China think the younger the tea leaves the better, so they pick the youngest little shoots. But,young tea shoots are by nature bitter to avoid insects from eating them. Taiwan tea makers pick the first two mature leaves, not only are they not as bitter, they also have time to absorb the fragrance of the surrounding flowering trees, such as in my case, orange blossom. You are probably familiar with the jasmine tea. It's poor grade tea with jasmine flowers added to try to imitate what a good tea should taste like naturally. I have here naturally flowery tea for you today from Taiwan." I started to pass around my ordinary tea from Taiwan in my teapot to let them smell it. Then I pour hot water from the ceramic water pot I had ready on the kerosene stove. After about one minute I pour it into a ceramic tea server so that everyone gets the same strength tea. In front of every guest there were two small cups, one smaller but taller "snifter" cup, the other bigger but shorter "drinking" cup. I first filled every snifter with tea, then everyone was supposed to pour it into the drinking cup and put the snifter to their nose to smell the fragrance. But there was this wise guy across from me, who turned out to be the owner of the most famous tea house in Moscow, he made a grand gesture of first covering his snifter with the drinking cup and then flipping both upside-down before taking the snifter to smell. It was obvious he wanted to show off that he knew something I didn't know. I noticed everyone was looking at him.

Tea Ceremony

After the first round, I said, "That's what we do ordinarily with ordinary tea. There are different schools of tea ceremony. Some emphasize the style, the steps and every move you make. I am pragmatic, I emphasize the content, You should first have good tea and do only necessary things to bring out the best in the tea. I don't do unnecessary acrobatics. Today we have very special guests here and I have brought the best tea from far away. I must show you the best way to make the best tea." So, I took out my tea toaster and said, "Tea leaves have a tendency to absorb it's surrounding orders. So, with the best tea, you need to use this toaster to expel whatever it picked up since it was made and then you have the freshly toasted tea with it's natural fragrance." Then I toasted my best tea on the fire gently for a minute and passed it around for everyone to smell the bad order. Afterward, I toasted it again for another minute and passed it around again. Everyone was amazed at how nice it smelled. Needless to say, they had not tasted such a good tea before, and the session was a big success. I noticed the wise guy was paying close attention and I must give him credit for recognizing he'd met his match, as he came up to me immediately after my demonstration and invited me for dinner and to visit his tea house. As it turned out he bought all the tea I brought along from Taiwan which paid for all our air tickets, including my wife and my brother's.

Carol was intrigued by my story and laughed at the story about the flipping of the teacups trick which she had just learned a few months ago attending another tea ceremony! We were getting along so well I thought I should move on to the next stage, so, I said, "Give me your hand, let me read your palm." She knew enough about Chinese culture and gave me her right hand, and I said, "You like beautiful things (she nodded), you're artistic (nodded again), you're not easy to mess with, if someone wrongs you, you'll hold a grudge for ever (nodded also)...... Actually you're very generous and will forgive those who have wronged you (nodding again), ...This is your lifeline. Oh, you'll get really sick at 65! But fortunately you'll get through it. You see, you have a long lifeline and will live a long life!......And this is your love line. A lot of people chase you, but you're very picky,....." She was amazed and said, "You can really read my mind!" and nudged closer to me. I put my arm over her shoulder and started to kiss her. We both undressed and I stood back to look at her whole body. What a beauty! She reminded me of the Greek marble statue of Venus.

Thinking back, I really regret asking her a stupid question and receiving a stupid answer which killed my appetite. Probably because I couldn't believe such beauty was willing to have sex with me, I asked, "I am curious Carol, there were so many nice men at the party why did you pick me?" She said, "I am very generous with my sex. I thought an old man like you would be really pleased to have a young girl like me." I swear, word for word that's exactly what she said. All I remember was that before I managed to say anything my penis instantly withered from ninety degrees to zero degrees. I was stunned by her answer and finally muttered, "Oops, you just said the wrong thing. I thought you liked me. I don't need charity. I have no problem finding young girls who like me!"

The Brain is the Most Important Sex Organ

I thought a lot about this failed one-night stand afterward. Why did I react so strongly and so quickly? I didn't mind her calling me an old man. I was in my mid-40s and she was in her early 20s, so, it's natural for her to regard me as old. What I objected to was her reason. Sex for charity? I had never heard of it before much less encountered it. My dignity was injured. Normally we think of sex as purely physical but now I realized it is also psychological or even spiritual. The brain is actually the most important sex organ! First of all, it's very important to me that I consider my sex partner beautiful.

That's esthetic consideration. Secondly, it's important to me she is doing it for the right reason. That's normative consideration.

Thirdly, it's important to me we are equal agents. That's moral consideration. This third consideration is especially important. We should not treat our sex partners as mere objects but as agents. That means mutual satisfaction is essential. Just to give an example. At one time I was trying to explain to my elder brother female sexual anatomy and how to give pleasure to women. He said, "Why do you worry about whether she enjoy it or not? You just do it to enjoy yourself, that's all." That's treating women just as sex objects and unfortunately, that was the prevailing male attitude in the old times. These are uniquely human considerations that place us apart from other animals. I want to go even further and say human sex is a spiritual experience. When I am kneeling between a beautiful woman's legs with my body joined to her and looking at her face, I feel so grateful that there is this creation who accepts me and shares this moment with me! Can any spiritual experience be better than that? Human sex has gone beyond the purely biological dimension.

Talking about failed one-night stands, there were many. Let me just go through a couple more examples. As a teacher, it's not uncommon for some students to be romantically interested in you. But I had a firm principle, I don't get romantically involved with anyone **while** she was my student. My reason is very simple. The teacher/student relationship is not equal. If a student comes on to you before the end of the course, you don't know whether she really likes you or just trying to exchange sex for a good grade. There was this really beautiful and lively student in one of my evening classes for part-time students. Laura was a retired air stewardess trying to get a college degree. She always sat in the front row paying attention and asking appropriate questions. She was a really good student and with a few other students, they would follow me after each class and invite me to continue the discussion in the university cafeteria.

That was OK with me but one time she said she wanted to take me to a nice private women's club for dinner. I said I didn't socialize with my students outside of the university campus and explained to her my principle, and said, "If you are really interested in me you can call me after the course is over and when I turn in my grade report." A week after I turned in my grade report, Laura called and invited me to dinner at her club.

Laura

The club was located in downtown Toronto. It had a beautiful sandblasted old-fashioned red brick facade but the interior was tastefully modernized with a swimming pool, sauna, exercise room, library, and restaurant. It was obviously a rich women's club. Laura showed me around fist before we sat down at a table overlooking the swimming pool. There were a lot of potted plants in this place which I liked. I hate any place decked with plastic trees and flowers which turns it from a possibly 5-stars place to a no-star place. Everything about this place was special. For example, I usually see roses, carnations, or chrysanthemums in fancy restaurant tables, but they had nasturtiums. As it turned out nasturtium butter was their specialty. It was the perfect match for the trout main dish I ordered. Ever since that meal I have been making my own nasturtium butter when the flower is in season. It's easily made, just finely chop fresh nasturtium flowers and mix them into soft butter. It goes so well with all fish dishes and even vegetables.

After the main dish, she asked if I wanted any dessert. I said, "No, I am already full." She said, "In that case we should just order the Irish coffee, it's their specialty." I thought I was just getting a cup of coffee but a waiter wheeled in front of us a fully equipped trolly. He first took out some coffee beans to let us smell them and said, this is Jamaican Blue Mountain coffee. It did smell good. Then he put them in a hand grinder to grind them and let us smell again. The aroma was fantastic. He put it in the percolator and turned on the stove. We patiently watched the coffee drip drop by drop until it was done. Meanwhile, the waiter took out two large brandy snifter glasses, wetted the rims, and dipped them in a plate of sugar so that there was a ring of sugar on each glass rim. The finished coffee was just enough for two glasses.

Finally, he poured in some Irish Cream whisky and flambéed it. While they were flaming he presented them to us and said, "Enjoy your coffee!" He was so proud of himself! The whole process was done with graceful choreographed steps that it was virtually a dance! I'd never seen anything like this before or after. Since then every time I go to a fancy restaurant or coffee house I asked if they have Irish coffee. They always say yes and I always get just a cup of coffee with a few drops of Irish cream.

Why isn't any place making real Irish Coffee? If I were younger I swear I would open an Irish Coffee House!

Then I realized why Laura wanted to take me to this place. She was really a good student. You see, the course I taught was on Daoism. The founder of this philosophy, Laoizi distinguished two kinds of human actions, actions with purposes and actions without purposes. The first kind regards your actions as means to end while the second kind regards your actions as ends in themselves. For example, if I fish for a living what I value is the end result, the fish or the money they can fetch. If you give me the same amount of fish or money I would rather not go fishing. But if fishing is your hobby, you enjoy the process of fishing itself. and even if someone gives you all the fish you want, you would still go fishing. The trick (or way, Dao, or art) of life is to reduce activities of the first kind and increase activities of the second kind.

His great disciple Zhuangzi, further developed this idea by showing that any activity, even the first kind, can be turned into the second kind if you adopt a proper attitude. He gave an example of a butcher who could carve up cow after cow for months with the same knife without needing to sharpen it because he knew his cows so well he never hit a bone. People gather to watch his performance, as he was proud of and enjoyed his work. He was cutting and slicing with his knife gracefully like a dancer. He turned a lowly messy job into an art form! Have you seen a Japanese film called "Departures" about a mortician turning a most unpleasant job into an art form?

Japanese are really good followers of Daoism, they can turn any activity into an art. On one of my trips to Japan, I saw s street vendor making waffles. He was totally absorbed in what he was doing, moving his hands rhythmically while humming a song.

He obviously was enjoying himself. That's the way to make waffles! The sex act obviously falls under the same Daoist classification: sex for reproduction belongs to the first kind, and sex for its own sake belongs to the second kind. To be human, we should increase the sex of the second kind, and turn it into an art form.

Thanks to Laura for showing me Irish Coffee, truly a good example of an ordinary activity turned into an art. That was definitely the best coffee experience I'd ever had. Laura really put her heart into planning this date. She booked a private room in the clubhouse for the afternoon. So. we moved to her room after dinner. It was tastefully decorated with fresh flowers and potted plants. Best of all there was a large jacuzzi tub behind the floor-to-ceiling glass partition. She went to turn the water on, and when it was half full she invited me to join her in the tub to relax. She also prepared two glasses of Grand Marnier to take to the jacuzzi. With liquor in hand, we got into the jacuzzi and she turned on the water massager. That was the first time I participated in such a decadent life. What a life!

I tried to find out more about her and asked, "Where do you live?" She said, "I live alone in the suburb with a big yard." I asked, "Don't you feel lonely living in a big place by yourself?" She said, "My two boys come home every weekend. Since my divorce I find I enjoy being by myself. I spend a lot of time gardening." I asked, "Do you have a steady male friend?" She said, "Not really, I do have a BTN." "What's that or should I rather ask who is that? I have never heard of that term," I asked. She said, "We girls call them 'Better Than Nothing'. They are handymen at our beck and call when we need them for odd jobs around the house or heavy work in the yard. Also when we have sexual needs." I said, "Oh, I am actually very handy myself and I would be happy to come and help, but I wouldn't want to be your BTN! It doesn't sound dignified." "No, no. I really like you and respect you. That's why I invite you here. I've never invited him here," she quickly replied. Then she turned serious and said, "Before we go on, I must tell you something. I have genital herpes.

It's a virus and not curable. Most of the time it has no symptoms and is not contagious, but when your immunity is low it flares up, and your genitals break out into blisters, and becomes very itchy. That's when you are most contagious. I am OK now, and I think it's the safe period." I said, "Thank you for being so honest. Actually I am very leery of transmittable diseases. I got hepatitis B once from one of my trips to Taiwan or China. I was very sick for months. I think we should be on the safe side. Actually I am perfectly satisfied already. The Irish Coffee alone really made my day. We should call it a day when we finish our Grand Marnier." Well, that was a glorious failed one-night stand. There were definitely more failed ones than successful ones. I will just tell one more to illustrate a wrong reason for sex. This was soon after I retired back to my home village in Taiwan in 1995. The owner of a nearby town grocery and I soon became good friends. As it turned out she was the most beautiful woman in the whole town and her husband was the ugliest man in town. His face was already ugly by regular standards, beady-eyed and buck-toothed. What's worst, due to a job accident, he was hunchbacked and could hardly walk. I asked how they got together? She said she was married to a good-for-nothing and abusive husband before and after giving birth to two children she decided to divorce him. But no available man would marry a divorced woman with two kids until she was introduced to this man. He was nice, hard-working, had a steady income, and was willing to take care of her two children.

Sex for Revenge

Thank heavens young women are more economically self-reliant now. I always tell my women students, never to give up their jobs and become economically dependent on their husbands. Economic independence is the basic condition for equality. Before this century, I dare say most women marry for economic reasons. Jade was a typical example. She sacrificed her sexuality for economic security. We got along really well, and knowing I was legally separated, she kept saying she wished we'd met earlier. I said it's best we kept a platonic relationship, having an affair with her would be too dangerous for me in a small town. So we were on our best behavior for many months, until one day she came to my house really upset and crying. I asked what happened?

She said, she came home yesterday afternoon and found her husband having sex on the couch with their foreign maid whom they hired to help take care of his old parents. I said, "You don't want to have sex with him any way, why are you so upset?" She said, "All these years I had a lot of men chasing after me, and I was sorely tempted sometimes, but always controlled myself, now he does this? I feel really betrayed!" That's really strange about marriage, you don't want to have sex with him, but he is not allowed to have it with anyone else! I said, "That's a good ground for divorce." She said. "I would like to, but I have to think about my economic situation." I said, "What are you going to do?" She said." I don't know. I just want to kill him!" I said, "Don't kill him. Get even!" She asked, how? I told her about what I did for revenge in a similar situation. She listened and stopped sobbing. I hugged her and suggested we should have sex, and she would feel much better. She seemed to agree while I lead her to my bedroom. We both undressed, and got on the bed. As I bent over to kiss her, she pushed me back and started crying again. I asked what's the matter? She said, "This is not right. That's not the way it should be. You see, you are my fantasy lover. I fantasized making love to you. I didn't want to have sex with you, because real sex may not be as good as my fantasy, or if it is really good, I may not be able to control myself, and that would jeopardize my marriage. If I make love with you it should be out of love, and not like this. I am full of negative feelings right now."

Well, that's really wise, and I couldn't agree more. I thanked her for saving me from committing another mistake, and we remained good friends to this day.

Leona

As to my mistake, it happened long long ago when I was young and stupid and stressed out. Like all breakups of long marriages, it was complicated and nasty and painful to recollect. One of the really unfortunate things about the divorce process is that the parties try to hurt each other as much as possible. At one point my wife tried to hurt me by sleeping with anyone she could lay her hands on and making sure I knew about it. I ask her why? She said she was doing it to humiliate me.

That's a new one! I couldn't understand until much later. All I could do at the time was to snap back," Don't bother! It's your body. You might as well enjoy yourself! Don't do it for me!" But it must have done something to me as I started to do something I was sure would hurt her. I started to date her best friend Linda. I knew she would accept me because of something that happened previous to my marriage breakup.

It was in the seventies during the time of anti-Vietnam war protests and the civil rights movement. A lot of young people, especially artists and musicians, were rebellious and anti-establishment. My wife was a musician and Leona was an artist.

They both came from upper-middle-class WASP families in the US. Politically they were left-liberals and culturally they considered themselves to be Hippies.

Leona lived just a couple of streets from us and we both have four children. So, they had much in common and the two families spent a lot of time together. She was married to a straight banker and she envied her best friend for having an exotic oriental professor as a husband. She was especially jealous of the fact that I did most of the cooking and spent a lot of time with my children. She said a number of times that she wished she'd married a Chinese. I said," Do you think all Chinese men are like that? You are committing a logical fallacy called hasty generalization. Because you know one Chinese who is like that and you generalize to think all Chinese are like that. Actually most Chinese men are male chauvinists like American men, may be even more so. I consciously reform myself because I believe in gender equality. You should give me credit for the way I am and not the whole Chinese race!"

At any rate, it was obvious she really liked me and she used every opportunity to show it. The funny thing was that when Leona gave me trinkets she made, my wife would pressure me to show more appreciation. because she said, it was important to Leona that I liked her things. I was forced to wear all kinds of bracelets and rings. Another strange thing that happened around that time was that one night, about an hour before my wife was to return home from a music lesson, Leona showed up at our house. Naturally I served some tea and chatted with her while waiting for my wife to return. It was during the time when Che Guevara was in the news and we got into a heated argument. I was strongly pro-revolution and she was against any form of violence. I was pretty annoyed at her and was relieved when I saw the clock showing it was a few minutes before my wife was due home. But she stood up quickly and said, "Oh, I'd better get going", and left. I thought that was a bit odd and didn't think any further.

As it turned out, they were both in their early 40's going through their mid-age crisis.

Unbeknownst to me (she told me later) my wife was complaining a lot about me to her. and she finally said, "If you don't want him, I want him!" She said my wife replied, "You can have him!" (Let that be a lesson to everyone. Don't complain about your spouse to your best friend, unless you really want to get rid of him!") Leona took it seriously. She divorced her husband and openly demanded my wife to give me up.

They created a lot of emotional scenes in the neighborhood. I had no clue what was going on, and my wife only told me Leona was having a nervous breakdown. When I finally realized what was going on, my wife accused me of leading her on. The truth was that I purposefully kept a distance from her and was not interested in her in the least. All that happened a couple of years before my marriage breakup.

After the breakup, my first thought was to see Leona. I said to her frankly, "I like you but I am not in love with you. I like to be your friend and have a sexual relationship but don't expect it to be a long term relationship. Any time you feel it's not OK, let me know." She told me what happened before. She said she didn't have a nervous breakdown. She was in love with me and she wanted my wife to keep her promise to give me up. The only thing she misjudged was that she thought I loved her. I asked what gave her that idea? She said she went by her vibes and she remembered what a wonderful discussion we had on Che Guevara. That goes to show you how different perspectives can give rise to totally different evaluations of the same event. She mulled over my proposal, and finally agreed to give it a try. We made a date the next evening at her house. Her living room was decorated in typical Hippie fashion, with no electric lights but a lot of candlelight and burning incense. The walls were covered with her wild paintings of animals and flowers. She was dressed in a colorful printed Indian blouse and long skirt with a headband. The whole ambiance was that of a cozy gypsy camp. I opened the Lagavulin, a Single Malt Scotch I brought along, which I knew she liked. We sipped our whisky.

and talked about the past and soon ended up in the bedroom.

Resurrection Hallucination

One thing that stood out in that encounter was my first hallucination experience. While I was on top of her pumping away, she suddenly "turned into my wife" in front of my eyes! There is no other way to describe the sense of reality I felt. Even her body felt like my wife's. I kept blinking my eyes, but she wouldn't go away. That was really terrifying!

It lasted for at least one minute. Later a good friend of mine told me he had the same experience while he was having sex with the mother of his estranged wife.

Actually, it's not an uncommon phenomenon. I think there should be a name for such a psychological state. i.e. hallucinating someone you really miss. "Resurrection Hallucination" would be a good name, since I believe the Bible story of Jesus's resurrection recorded the oldest cases of this form of hallucination. I remember reading Luke's Gospel, there were two disciples on their way to a village while discussing the crucifixion of their master Jesus the day before. They were joined by someone they didn't recognize.

When they reached the village at dusk, they invited him to join them for dinner. While eating, under the dim light, they suddenly recognize him as Jesus. As the Bible has it: "Then their eyes were opened, and they recognized him, and he disappeared from their sight." That's a typical hallucination!

What about other witnesses, sometimes hundreds of them, who were sure they had seen and talked to him in flesh? They were no doubt honestly reporting their experiences, but unlike dreams, hallucinations feel so real! Remember, they were Jesus's devote disciples who not only miss him hugely but also fervently believe he would "arise on the third day". It's only natural he would "appear" to them, say things they were expecting to hear, and then "disappear from their sight". As the Bible has it:" While he was blessing them, he left them and was taken up into heaven." That's a typical mass hallucination.

Leona and I dated a few times. It was quite nice at the beginning. We were good friends, and we satisfied each other's sexual needs. But her Hippie lifestyle wasn't really my cup of tea. For one thing, she liked to smoke, both cigarettes and marihuana, but I don't like either. I think her frequent smoke of marihuana was the cause of her skewed sense of reality. Even while we were making love she would have the whiskey in one hand and the cigarette or marihuana in another. The combined smell was not conducive to intimate activity, to say the least. So, I don't kiss her. What's more disturbing was that she didn't believe in disciplining her children. They would come in and out of the bedroom and ask her for things while we were in the bed. In addition, she didn't take good care of her body. She might have been quite beautiful in her youth, but after four kids she was definitely over the hill. Her big breasts were drooping down to her navel and whenever she was on top of me they would suffocate me. I was just about to tell her I did not wish to continue our relationship when she told me she would like me to meet her family.

Another total miss-perception of the situation. She must've thought everything was going fine.

So, I told her she was getting too serious, and I wanted to break off our relationship.

I was raped

My brief fling with Leona occasioned an unexpected reaction from my wife, which I don't understand to this day. After we separated and she moved out, she would come back once in a while to see the kids. One evening she came to see them after supper, and after they went upstairs to go to bed, she said she wanted to talk with me.

We went to the living room, and she poured herself a big glass of brandy (Which I know from my experience with her is a danger sign). We sat down on the rug in front of the fireplace. She didn't beat around the bush and immediately asked, "You are sleeping with Linda, aren't you?" I shoot back, "I don't ask you with whom you are sleeping. You don't want to sleep with me, and whom I am sleeping with is none of your business." I fully expected yelling, shouting, kicking, hitting, and throwing things at me as she used to do. But something unfathomable happened; she took a big gulp of the brandy and said, "I don't know why but the thought of you having sex with somebody else really excited me!" That's another new one from her! What a perverted lady, I thought to myself. What happened next, I can only say, "I was raped by my wife!" By that time, I certainly did not want sex with her, especially that day. That morning I was with May, and in the afternoon, I was with Betty. Twice in a day is about my limit. I was not prepared for the third time in one day. That was definitely forced upon me, and I remember only two things. One, I had rug burns again on my elbows. Second, once more, I proved to myself that my body reacts differently to different partners. Within the same day, my penis behaved differently with different women: medium-hard with May, hardest with Betty, and barely erect with my wife. Your body's preference is perfectly clear.

Why do I call it "rape"? Some people may think there is no such thing as a woman raping a man. That's simply not true. Rape is sex imposed on you when you do not want it. That can happen either way and even though, in reality, most victims are women. That is because of their weaker position vis-à-vis the men/women power relationship. If a woman is in a more powerful position, she can rape men also. To give you an example, my ex-wife's brother was psychologically in a mess.

When he visited us, I noticed him putting a knife under his pillow to sleep and asked him why? He said he was afraid of being raped by women. I said, "You are a strong 6-foot tall man. Why are you afraid of being raped by women?" I paused for a while and knowing his family background, I asked, "Did your adopted mother rape you when you were small?" He was really surprised and said, "How do you know?" I said, "I don't need to be Freud to figure out that the only reason a strong man has a fear of being raped by women is if he was sexually molested by a woman when he was small and helpless."

He and his sister, my ex-wife, had a nightmarish childhood, which scarred them for life. Their natural parents got divorced when they were six and eight, and they were put in an orphanage. A few years later, they were adopted by a supposedly respectable, church-going couple. She was a primary school teacher, and he was a state representative; but in reality, they were rotten to the cord. I found out about their horrible story slowly through her, what seemed to me, strange behaviors. First, she hated her adopted parents, and I hadn't met anyone who hated their parents so much, adopted or otherwise. Secondly, before we made love, she would inebriate herself with alcohol. Initially, I thought she enjoyed a little wine and liquor like me and bought expensive French brandy, like Cognac.

Soon I found out she wasn't into wine tasting but just needed the alcohol to intoxicate herself. As she needed about half a bottle to reach that state each time, I realized I couldn't afford to supply her with the expensive stuff. So, I stocked up with cheap Spanish brandy. And to prove me right, she never complained. However, even with the numbing effect of the alcohol, she was still tense when I approached her for sex. I finally asked one time, "Why don't you just relax?" She shot back, "That's what *all men* said!" I was shocked and muttered," I am not *all men*, I am your husband, and I love you." Then, I asked," Who are *all men*?" She finally told me about her horrendous childhood, growing up in a household in which not only her so-called father but uncles also abused her sexually. I asked," Why didn't you tell your mother?" she said," I did; she not only didn't believe me but also beat me up for lying!" As it turned out, she was another devil who sexually molested her adopted boy!

Anyone going through that kind of childhood is psychologically damaged for life. I don't know whether psychotherapy is advanced enough to help them now. But, in our time, it seemed impossible. He was tall, handsome, smart, and college-educated, but he could never hold on to a job or stay put in one place. He was typical of schizophrenia, who was always running away from his presumed enemy. The problem was that he had an unshakable conspiracy theory which may be quite dangerous if it included you as a co-conspirator. That reminds me of a tragedy that killed a woman I was about to date.

You see, pottery was one of my hobbies, and one year my college arranged to have an exhibit of my works before Christmas.

Afterward, my secretary told me that a new woman faculty asked if I would sell her a few pieces. She especially liked turquoise glazed ones. "Was it Tania, the gorgeous Ukrainian new Ph.D. who just joined the history department?" I asked. My secretary said yes. That's great, as I had my eyes on her since she came and was trying to find an opportunity to approach her. So, I took a few turquoise pieces and went over to her office. She asked, how much do they cost? I said, "No charge for you, regard it as a ' get acquaintance gift' according to Chinese custom, as I wanted to get acquainted with you since you came." She said she liked the Chinese custom, but she would like to give me a Christmas gift in return, according to Western custom. I said, "I would like nothing better than a date with you. Would you like to come to my house one day, and I will do the Chinese tea ceremony with my own pottery handmade tea set?" She said, "That sounds great, and I am looking forward to it, but it has to be after Christmas since we have a family get-together scheduled for Christmas." So, we set our date a few days after Christmas, on the 28th. But, on the 26th, there was big tragic news all over the papers that a Ukrainian family of six was killed by a schizophrenic family member, her brother!

What shocking news! I was devastated. I had placed so much hope in this relationship, and now it's gone like a dream. The last time my wife's brother visited, it was a bit scary, as he kept asking me why I was following him thousands of miles away in Florida, Arizona, California, etc.

No amount of reassuring him that I never left Toronto was going to change his mind because he 'saw' me with his own eyes! He was deep into his conspiracy theory and left with great fear. After that, we never heard from him again. Certainly, he did not have a good ending.

As to my relationship with my wife, it can only be called a tragedy by looking back calmly and rationally. She was beautiful, intelligent, talented, kind-hearted, but insecure. On a personal level, we got along quite well. We had four beautiful, wonderful, and talented kids. All our friends regarded us as a model family and an ideal couple.

Nevertheless, her deep-seated insecurity was hanging over our marriage like the Sword of Damocles. She was convinced nothing good was going to last; she was going to be abandoned suddenly one day as her parents did. She was not happy, no matter what I did. No amount of love, four kids, and eighteen years of marriage could convince her of otherwise. Like a self-fulfilling prophecy, she finally did things to make sure her deepest fear came true. What can I say? I can only try to learn from my experience, and henceforth, every time I meet a prospective partner, my first question is, "Were you ever abandoned by either of your parents?"

Gale

I don't want to go too much into my marriages and long-term relationships now. After finishing this book, and if I still have time and energy, maybe I will write another book to be called. "My Love Affairs." For now, I want to finish this book by telling one more strange one-night stand with Gale. I met her at one of my Jiaozi parties. She was overly made-up for my taste, but she was pretty, and above all, she was interested in birds, a special hobby of mine. I am a full-fledged aviculturist with life-long experience in keeping and breeding rare birds, especially parrots. I kept hundreds of them in my basement: Some common ones like cockatiels, rosellas, lories, amazons, and some rare ones like Eclectus, hyacinth macaws, thick-billed parrot, fig parrots, black-billed amazon, kookaburras, and rarest of them all, a St.Vincent amazon.

I could talk to a bird lover for hours. Actually, she was only interested in buying a cheap bird for a pet, and I recommended a cockatiel.

So, that weekend I picked a nice tame male cockatiel with orange cheeks and delivered it to her apartment. She loved it and bounded with it immediately. But she started thinking he might be too lonesome when she went to work. She thought she should get a female to keep him company. I said," Don't be in such a hurry. See how you do with one bird first." She wanted to come to my place to see my setup and then decide whether she could breed birds also.

She came that weekend was really impressed by my aviary, and decided to breed birds as a hobby. She did think it was a good idea to start small and bought a female cockatiel.

She was equally impressed by my greenery in the living room. Growing up in Taiwan, I am semi-tropical and really missed greenness in the dreary Toronto winter. So, I have a lot of potted plants in my living room. She couldn't believe what she saw and said," Others may have a few plants in their living rooms, but you have a jungle here! I love plants too, but I have a hard time keeping them alive. You must have a green thumb!" I said," It has nothing to do with the color of your thumbs. Most likely, you loved them to death. You either give them too much water or fertilizer." Then, I gave her a lesson on how to take care of indoor plants. You need to give indoor plants three things: sunlight, water, and soil. But, you need to know what not to do first: no fertilizer and not too much water! Fertilizers, especially chemical ones, are too strong. It will kill them. Too much water will drown them by causing root rot. Make sure the drip pan beneath each pot is completely dry before you water again. The only other thing you need to know is to take the plants out of their pots every spring, cut out the overgrown roots that are choking them and then replace the cutout parts with new soil. If you follow these simple steps, you will have a green thumb too.

We really got along very well, as we shared many common interests, and she obviously liked me. So, since it was getting dark, I said, "Why don't you stay for supper?" She said she would be happy to, but she didn't want me to go into any trouble. I said," No problem, I can whip up something quick and simple." No kidding, I like cooking and can prepare a decent meal for a small group within half an hour. So, I went to work immediately:

1. I got some frozen peeled shrimps from the freezer, put them directly on a shallow pan, sprinkled some garlic powder and black pepper, poured liquified butter over them, and then put it in the oven and turned on the grill.
2. I cut up some zucchini, tomato, red and green pepper, and onion; put them all in a frying pan with olive oil, sprinkle a lot of garlic powder and Italian seasoning, and then stir fry them.
3. I set up the dining table with French bread, nasturtium butter, and special avocado salad. It's a simple but most delicious way to eat the avocado I learned from a Cuban girlfriend. You cut a ripe avocado in half, take the big seed out, fill each middle space with fresh lemon juice, sprinkle the whole top with a lot of freshly minced garlic and a little salt and pepper, then spoon it out to eat.
4. When the shrimp were done, I took it out and poured over it a little sherry, and placed it on the table. Meanwhile, the Italian vegetable was done, and we were ready for supper!

The whole thing took less than half an hour. Gale watched the entire process in amazement; she couldn't believe they were so delicious and wanted to know how to make each dish. We accompanied the whole meal with a bottle of Chablis Premier Cru. Speaking of Chablis, when I went to the U. S. in the 1950s, every white wine was called Chablis, every red wine was called Burgundy, and every sparkling wine was called Champagne! Luckily, an international place of origin law was put in place later to regulate brand names of products. When I got into wine tasting, I soon realized the best white wine came from Chablis, the best red from Burgundy, and the best bubbly from Champagne. That's why those names were widely misused.

Transsexuality

After supper, we took the remaining Chablis back to the living room and sat down on the Persian rug in front of the fireplace. After we finished the bottle, she said." I think I have too much wine to drive home." I said," You mean you want to stay overnight here?" She said," If you don't mind." So, I said, "OK, I'll go upstairs to take a shower, and you can take yours downstairs."

I am a slow bather. By the time I finished and came downstairs, she was already fully dressed and waiting for me in front of the fireplace. A shocking sight presented itself in front of me. With her makeup washed away and without her false eye-lashes, she appeared to be an entirely different person. Luckily, she merely dropped from "pretty" to "pleasant" in my grading system, which was still a passing grade.

Being a teacher, I have a bad habit of grading women's looks in a grading system: pleasant (60%, C). Pretty (70%, B), beautiful (80%, A-), gorgeous (90%, A) and exquisite (100%.A+). I can only have sexual relationships with women I consider at least "pleasant."

I didn't say anything about her looks and went to get a bottle of Talisker single malt whisky. We continued discussing wine-tasting in my Tatami room. After a while, she started to cuddle up to me, and I put my arm around her shoulder. Soon, we started kissing each other; I reached the wall switch to dim the light, but she wanted it completely dark. So, we started undressing each other; and that's when I began to sense something was not kosher. Usually, women have more under-skin fat than men, making them naturally softer than men, but she felt hard. Then, I asked, as I usually do," Are you protected?" She gave an unexpected answer," You don't have to worry. It would be a miracle if I got pregnant because I don't have a uterus." I was so stunned that it didn't occur to me to ask why. I instinctively reached for her breasts, but there weren't any to speak of, and then I reached down to see if she had a vagina. She did, but when I tried to find the clitoris, there wasn't any, and her vagina was dry. So, I lubricated my penis with my saliva and managed to put it inside her.

However, unlike other vaginas, which were soft and yielding inside, hers was tight all the way. It suddenly occurred to me; I was having sex with a transsexual! I lost interest immediately and said," I am tired, let's sleep."

I reflected on transsexuality carefully after that incident, and here is my analysis. We are born male or female; that's our sex.

Nature designed us differently for the division of labor in procreation.

Through evolution, different characteristics developed in the sexes, which were beneficial for the survival of the species. First of all, women's relative immobility during pregnancy and childcare period require assistance from men.

Secondly, the most important determining factor in the development of these characteristics was the way of procuring food. When the gathering was the main method of procuring food, there was probably not a big difference between the size and strength of men and women. As hunting became more important, men became bigger, stronger, more aggressive, more adventuresome, more out-going, etc. In contrast, women were smaller, weaker, gentler, more conservative, more domestic, etc. These characteristics are called masculinity and femininity; that's our gender. Originally a statistical generalization: most men are masculine, and most women are feminine, later became a social demand: all men should be masculine, and all women should be feminine. However, not all men are born masculine; and not all women are born feminine.

Traditionally society has a strong method of enforcing the social demand from the day you were born. Have you ever wondered why the first question everyone asks at a baby's birth is: "Boy or girl?" You may say we want to know what name to call them, what toys to give them, what dresses to buy them, etc. But why the difference? The answer is that the adults want to know whether a newborn baby is a boy or a girl so that they know how to treat them. There are social processes of, what I call, "genderization" to turn girls into feminine women and boys into masculine men. It's virtually a brainwashing process; it accepts no deviation. Traditionally, this social pressure is overwhelming. We want boys to be strong, active, independent, aggressive, extroverted, etc. so that they can grow up to be heads of families and leaders in society. At the same time, we want girls to grow up to be weak, passive, reliant, gentle, introverted, etc., so that they can grow up to be good wives and mothers. They are expected to become two antithetical and opposite kinds of human beings. Non-conformers suffer grave consequences. If you are a girl but not feminine enough according to the social demand, you are called a "tomboy." Contrarily, if you are a boy but not masculine enough, you are called "sissy." Both terms are derogatory and psychologically damaging to the individual. Non-conforming individuals growing up under the genderization juggernaut are likely to think there is something wrong with themselves. They feel there is a mismatch between their body (sex) and their spirit or soul (gender); they would prefer to be the other sex. These people are called transsexuals. One way of coping with the perceived problem is to join the other sex by cross-dressing. However, this is merely cosmetic. The present gender differences in clothing, hairstyles, and makeup are entirely cultural and can vary from time to time and from place to place. Furthermore, if there were no gender differences in clothing, how does a man dress like a woman? It is not even possible.

A more extreme form of adjustment is to change your body by plastic surgery. I suspect Gale belonged to this group. This kind of solution is really tragic. It's like: if there were only two sizes of shoes to choose from, and if you don't find a pair that fits your feet, you trim your feet to fit it. Your sex is given by nature and can not be changed. If a man mutilates himself and uses surgery to make himself look like a woman, he is still not a woman; he is merely a castrated man. He cannot orgasm or give birth to children. What is needed is not trimming your feet, but changing shoe sizes. Both coping strategies are misguided as they are directed towards the symptoms and not the disease. The disease is social and not individual; it's genderization. There is nothing wrong with a man feeling "feminine" or a woman feeling "masculine".

You need not and should not accept the social demand.

Genderization may have served humans well in the past when brute force was vital for the survival of the species. But, in the modern world, brute force is not only no longer necessary but has also become a hindrance to the modern way of life. It's high time we stop genderization and replace it with equality of the sexes. We should stop bringing up two kinds of people with opposite characteristics along sexual lines, and start bringing up both sexes to be "good" people with the same set of qualities like gentle, caring, compassionate, independent, self-reliant, etc.; incorporating good qualities from both genders. In this ideal society, there will still be "feminine" men and "masculine" women, but they won't feel there is any problem because society accepts them.

Western feminism

Speaking of equality of the sexes, I want to point out a major mistake in the predominant Western way of thinking.

Feminism became a big social movement in the West during the mid-twentieth century.

Its battle cry was: "Women can and should do whatever men are doing!" If that means, "Equal pay for equal work," for example, no one can disagree with that. But if it means women should also do some stupid things men do, such as boxing, that's another story. We regard rooster fighting, dog fighting, and bullfighting as barbaric; why watching two men knocking each other out is not barbaric? In a more civilized society, boxing should be banned. For women to gain the right to fight in boxing is not what equality is all about!

I met a woman libber who proudly told me," I don't cook!" as if that's a badge of women's liberation. That's plain stupidity.

The inability to cook for yourself is nothing to be proud of, in men or women. It is true that in the traditional family, men don't cook; only women cook; that's wrong. The solution is not for women to stop cooking but for men to learn to cook also.

To put it more succinctly, a lot of feminists think of equality as emulating men; which means the masculinization of females.

However, what is needed is the feminization of males. Here, I think, we could use some input from Daoism. Its great founder, Laozi said 2500 years ago." Hard and strong are companions of death. Soft and gentle are companions of life." (*Dao De Jing*, Sect. 76) Unlike the mainstream Western philosophy which gives priority to masculinity, Daoism extols femininity as a superior human quality and masculinity as detrimental to human life. In fact, statistics tell us, women live five to seven years longer than men on average. There are no known biological reasons for this discrepancy. The most reasonable culprit is masculinity. From childhood, we tell boys to be strong, brave, and not to cry so that they can grow up to fight in wars, do hard and risky work, and take high-pressure jobs; all are "companions of death" according to Laozi. No wonder men end up having a shorter lifespan.

There is another aspect of masculinity I wish to remind my male friends who may secretly harbor the thought, "Men are superior is society now; why give up a good thing?" You not only have a shorter lifespan, but also you are missing out on the most important thing in life—your children's love. How? You may ask. In China, there is a phrase that summarizes the traditional roles in parenting: "Father, stern; mother, kind." Father was the disciplinarian while mother was the nurturer in the family. Now you tell me who do you like better, the disciplinarian or the nurturer? I taught my philosophy of sex course in Canada for many years; and during the first few years I asked my students," Tell me honestly who do you love most, your father or your mother?" I got almost 100% reply, "mother!" Afterward, I didn't need to ask anymore.

You see, the love of your mother is natural;

she gave birth to you, she nurtured you, she is with you all the way. "Fatherhood" is a new and relatively recent concept in human history. It came into being only about 10,000 years ago with the rise of agriculture and patriarchy. For millions of years before that, we live in matriarchy; in which we knew only who our mothers were and not our natural fathers. Children's love for their fathers is not "natural" but cultural; it needs to be cultivated. The traditional fathers were foolish to play the stern disciplinarian role and ended up lonely in their old age. I have even seen a few who were literally abandoned. In one case, I had a friend who lived in Japan for 70 years and raised five kids with the old militaristic method, fashionable before the Second World War.

As the parents got older, their children took care of both of them; but after the mother died, they found it "inconvenient" to take care of their Alzheimer-ridden father of eighty and sent him back to Taiwan for his extended family to take care of him. Luckily, he had a few younger brothers who took care of him for another ten years until he died. So, my sincere advice to young fathers is: Wise up; cultivate your children's love for you; you have to earn it! Don't let your wife tell the kid who has done wrong,"Wait until your father gets home, he will punish you!" Refuse to be the bad guy.

Tell her to do the punishment herself on the spot when it is most effective. You should bring home candies and goodies so that they will look forward to your coming home instead of dreading it! Kidding aside, here we really need the feminization of the masculine. You should learn to be a mother. I was smarter early on. I changed diapers, I woke up during the night to bottle feed them, I cooked three meals, I send and pick them up from schools, and I tell them good night stories. After my divorce, I single-handedly took care of my four kids for eight years. I earned a good relationship with all my children.

Homosexuality

Next, I would like to discuss a related but different topic, that of homosexuality.

Transsexuality is caused by gender confusion but homosexuality is based on sexual preference. They are entirely different matters. I will give an example to illustrate my point. After one of my classes in which I discussed these issues, a girl came up to me and said," I live with a girlfriend whom I call 'husband'. I thought we were homosexuals.

Now I am confused." I said," Bring her along next week." So, she did. My student was petite and very "feminine" while her "husband" was a head taller, dressed in army uniform, and had a crew cut; obviously trying to look very masculine. Afterward, I asked her," If you two break up one day, will you look for a man or a woman to be your husband?" She said, a man. I said," Then, neither of you is homosexual. You are a heterosexual who love this person as a man, and she is a transsexual who loves you thinking she is a man."

A true homosexual is someone who is sexually attracted to the same sex. Let me tell you another story to illustrate my point. There was a movie about two women, "A" and "B", living together in a love relationship. They got along really well, but one day "B" saved up enough money and went abroad to get plastic surgery to make her body look like a male. That was her dream coming true; but when she returned home, instead of congratulating her for realizing her dream, "A" immediately broke off their love relationship. "B" couldn't understand and asked," I am still the same person. Why are you dumping me?" What happened was inevitable. "A" was a homosexual who fell in love with "B" with a woman's body.

"B" was a transsexual whose dream was to become a man. Once she realized her dream, "A" lost interest. Their relationship was built on a pretense. I suspect most of what the public recognizes as "homosexual relationships" are of the above kind, especially where you can identify a clear gender role.

A true homosexual relationship cannot be identified outwardly; I learned that very early in my life. The first school I attended was a small Mennonite college, and one of my American roommates was a homosexual.

One night, he came to my bed while I was getting ready to sleep; and said he was a homosexual and that if I were interested he would like to make love to me. I said I wasn't interested, and that was that, and he never bother me again. Later, I was curious who else in the college were homosexuals. He pointed out everyone he knew to me, more than ten of them; and I was surprised none of them fitted my previous stereotypical conception of homosexuals as "effeminate". They were all athletic and masculine; in fact, some of them were on the college football team, including my roommate. That's when I realized homosexuals are sexually attracted to people like themselves; males are attracted to male bodies and females to female bodies. Homosexuality was traditionally considered abnormal, unnatural, irreligious, immoral, and unaesthetic. It's incredible that a single human activity can be labeled with so many serious accusations at the same time. I can think of no other. Let me analyze each of these accusations.

"It's not normal."

Normality is a statistical concept. What the majority does is called normal, but it does not imply it is necessarily good. A lot of good things are not normal, for example, geniuses. Homosexuals are not normal because they belong to the minority, so what?

"It's unnatural."

In one sense of "natural", it's true nature made the two sexes for reproduction; but if that's all sex is for. we need to engage in sex only two or three times in a lifetime. As I emphasized, human sex is divorced from reproduction. Given the overpopulation problem the world is facing, we should encourage non-productive sex instead of ostracizing it. A lot of things are not natural; they are cultural, but they are not necessarily bad.

In another sense of "natural", everything that happens in nature is natural.

Homosexuality does occur in nature; I have seen it in animals on my farm. However, not everything that happens in nature is necessarily good, for example, earthquakes and hurricanes.

So, the arguments," Homosexuality is bad because it is unnatural," or "Homosexuality is good because it is natural," are both irrelevant.

"It's irreligious."

Christians believe it's God's command that sex is for reproduction and any deviation from it is wrong. A good thing is that non-believers don't have to abide by a religious command; but in the Christian-dominated society, you are constantly facing religious values being imposed on the larger community. It's an ongoing struggle, not only on homosexuality but also on contraception and especially on abortion.

"It's immoral."

What is moral and what is immoral? The answer is quite simple: an action is moral if it benefits people, and action is immoral if it harms people. Homosexuality is a private sexual activity that benefits the participants and harms no one; why is it deemed immoral?

"It's unaesthetic."

Beauty is in the eyes of the beholder. It's just a matter of personal taste. For the world of me, I don't understand why some people like blue cheese or "stinky tofu"; but that does not give me any right to stop them or ostracize them.

In summary, none of the above accusations hold any water. Homosexuality is a private matter. It's none of anybody's business.

Society shouldn't have any say about it. It should be taken out of social and political discourses.

To fight against homophobia, homosexuals and their friends have launched a pretty successful social and political movement in the West, which has coalesced into the LGBT movement in recent years. The goal of this kind of political movement is to enact laws to protect their rights. However, I see some problems with this approach. First of all, lumping lesbians, gays, bisexuals, and transexuals together is a mistake. The first three refer to their sexual preferences but the fourth is a matter of gender confusion and not sexual preference.

Transsexuality will disappear with the disappearance of genderization. Before that happens we should educate individuals to stand up to the social pressure of genderization. I have successfully helped a number of students and relatives myself.

Secondly, the solution through legislation may not be the best thing in the long run. I will try to explain.

Same-sex Marriage

One legal right homosexuals try to gain is same-sex marriage. Only recently Taiwan passed a law to allow it. As it was the first country in the East to pass such a law it was touted as great progress. I beg to disagree and my reasons need to be carefully explained. You see, I am an anarchist in matters related to sex; I think governments should butt out of people's private sexual lives altogether. The most powerful control society has over peoples' sexual lives is through the institution of marriage. As I have argued again and again. monogamy is a bad institution. I am not opposed to one-to-one sexual relationships for life if you are lucky enough and happy enough, but I oppose it as an institution imposed on everyone. I think it should be abolished and replaced by the concept of friendship. Friendship is not a legal institution: it's a flexible and tolerant concept. You can have any number of friends for any length of time: all depending on your mutual need. My ideal sexual relationship is a mutually beneficial relationship between equals. A homosexual relationship seems to be a good example.

Why do homosexuals want to give up a perfectly good thing and join the terrible heterosexual marriage institution?

A Few Final Words

In the past, because sex was so tied up with procreation, society naturally steps in to control it tightly. However, with the coming of modern contraception, abortion, and over-population, it's time for society to cease interfering with people's private sexual activities. Sex, instead of being a social and political issue, should become purely a private and health matter only. The best thing in the future is to abolish marriage altogether. Failing that, and before marriage as an institution disappears naturally, individuals can reclaim their natural human rights by freeing themselves from all the past indoctrination. You just need to find a willing partner and make sure you don't get unwanted pregnancy and transmittable sexual disease. Everything else is nobody's business. It's strictly a private affair between you two. All my one-night stands were not known to anyone else to this day. Even in the most restrictive social situation, some people managed to breakthrough. Luckily, society is much more open now in comparison to my days, but it still has a long way to go before full sexual liberation. As to myself, I actually find it a big relief to be freed from sexual desire. Also, with very little physical activity, I need little food and hence never feel hungry. There is nothing pulling me from outside, neither food nor women. I finally feel like a free human being without any desires, ambitions, dreams, or fears, especially fear of death. My mind is in a state of "dead ashes "(Zhuangzi), or "Nothingness" (Laozi), or "emptiness" (Buddhism). Isn't that what Daoists and Buddhists try to achieve through meditation?

I am at peace with myself and with the world. However, my stroke paralyzed my right side which is subjected to relentless gravitational pull and makes me feel unbalanced when I stand up. If I were granted one last wish, I would like to spend three months in the gravitation-free space station and then walk out of the cabin and become a cosmic dust circling the earth.

20211110 at Thumb-up Garden

About the Author

K. T. Fann, now retired, was formerly Professor and Chair of Philosophy at Atkinson College, York University, Canada. He is the author of *Wittgenstein's Conception of Philosophy* (1969), *Pierce's Theory of Abduction* (1970), *Reading " Dao De Jing" in English* (2020), *In Praise of One-night Stand* (2021); editor of *Wittgenstein: The Man and His Philosophy* (1967) and *Symposium on J. L. Austin* (1969); and translator of *Laozi's Dao De Jing* (2020). In 1995 he retired to his ancestral village in Taiwan and turned a one-hectare abandoned farm into a self-sufficient Daoist retreat, where he lives a life of simplicity in harmony with nature and manages a Daoist retreat called Thumb-up B&B.

CPSIA information can be obtained
at www.ICGtesting.com
Printed in the USA
BVHW091149200922
647493BV00009B/922